Crescent Books
New York

Pictures supplied by:

Anglo-E.M.I./The National Film Archive: p. 114
B.B.C. Broadcasting: pp. 21, 22, 23, 60, 61, 85
The British Museum: p. 12
Bulloz: pp. 16, 105
Bruce Coleman: p. 18
Bologne, Polozzo Pogg: p. 20
Bruten: p. 87
Columbia -Warner/The National Film Archive: pp. 8, 9, 58
C.I.C./The National Film Archive: pp. 59, 63, 83, 84
Cinema Bookshop: p. 75
Eros/The National Film Archive: pp. 46, 47
Fox-Rank/The National Film Archive: pp. 4, 102
Hammer Films: p. 82
Kobal Collection: pp. 14, 19, 26, 27, 28, 36, 38, 39, 54, 62, 107, 108, 111, 113
Marvel Comics/Transworld: pp. 5, 10, 35, 50, 57, 81, 95, 100
Mansell Collection: pp. 6, 73

Musee de Gustav Moreau: pp. 16, 96, 105
Mary Evans Picture Library: pp. 32, 55, 69, 74, 88, 115
National Gallery p. 25
National Film Archive: p. 20
Popperfotos: p. 71, 117, 119
Purnell Books p. 13
Radio Times Hulton Picture Library: pp. 15, 24, 30, 31, 33, 40, 41, 42, 43, 44, 45, 49, 51, 65, 75, 80, 89, 90, 92, 93, 106, 109.
Regal International: p. 52, 91
R.K.O./The National Film Archive: pp. 67, 68, 77
Royal Geographical Society: p. 116
Scala: p. 17
Spectrum Colour Library: pp. 27, 98, 99, 104, Title page
Star Trek/Gene Roddenberry: p 97
United Artists Corporation: p. 110
William MacQuitty: p. 7

Acknowledgements
To Dan Bowling, Monster-boy,
and with special thanks to
Toby-Stuart Jervis.

Distributed to the trade by
Crescent Books, a division of Crown Publishers, Inc.

Copyright © 1974 by Marshall Cavendish Publications Limited

First Printing 1974

Second Printing 1975

Library of Congress Catalog Card Number 74-78077

ISBN 0-517-138786

Printed in Great Britain

This edition not to be sold outside the U.S.A. or Canada.

Introduction

Monsters – both real and fictitious – have always
been a focal point of man's curiosity.

From the depths of his imagination, man has
created terrible beasts and hideous hybrid
creatures, and legends describe spirits and demons
of dreadful appearance and appalling deeds that
have stalked the world.

Even without the assistance of imagination, pre-
history has given us huge animals of gargantuan
size and grotesque appearance.

Despite centuries of progress and technology,
monsters show no signs of dying out. The
television picture, the horror movies and the
multi-media of science fiction are constantly
creating new monsters to terrify us and chill the
blood. And modern discoveries have been made,
in the depths of the oceans and in little known
corners of the world, that show us that there are
still unknown horrors to be discovered.

This illustrated book describes all the real and
un-real monsters known to man, from A to Z. So
come with us now and journey through the dark
side of your imagination and reality, paying a visit
to the horrific world of monsters.
If you dare.

Achelous

His beard was long and intertwined with the dark undergrowth of the river bed, and from it water streamed continually. His clothes were fashioned from the green river weeds. His name was *ACHELOUS*, the river god of Greek mythology.

He was able to change his shape at will, from this his normal guise to horrendous and monstrous forms. Sometimes he was seen as a vile and hideously speckled serpent, at others, as a fierce stamping bull.

In his famous confrontation with the hero Hercules, Achelous assumed the hybrid form of a man with the head of a bull. In the closely

below: One of the patients who received the serum and his transformation into an Alligator person.

fought battle that followed, Hercules smote the horn from the head of the monster with one desperate blow. Achelous screamed with pain, as the blood which flowed from the wound, made red the murky waters of the river. Legend has it that every drop of this unnatural blood gave rise to a Siren, the mysterious women whose strange songs lured many seamen to their deaths on the jagged rocks. Hercules snatched up the horn and it is said that the horn itself later became the fabled Cornucopia or horn of plenty.

Alligator People

No-one suspected that the serum could produce such diabolical side-effects. The experiment was intended to help mankind and yet it produced some of the most terrifying mutants the world of science-fiction movies could invent . . . the *ALLIGATOR PEOPLE* . . .

The serum had been distilled from alligator fluids, and it was designed to enable the maimed victims of accidents to grow new limbs. However, as the anguished doctors looked on in horror, the limbs of their patients became the terrible clawed forelegs and feet of the alligator.

Yet more horrors were to come as their skin changed to green and slimy scales, and they began to form the heads and deadly crushing jaws of the alligator. Bewildered and enraged, these semi-reptilian monsters began to prey upon their fellow humans, until finally they suffered the fate of so many man-made monsters before them, their destruction by those responsible for their demise.

Allosaurus

Imagine a creature thirty-five feet long with the general appearance of a badly proportioned lizard. The hind legs were strong, large and well-developed, with three big clawed toes. The front legs, however, were quite small, with similar clawed 'fingers'. The creature's head was enormous, with the jaws and terrible sharp teeth of a crocodile. Such a beast sounds like the ultimate fantasy of a horror movie maker, but it really lived on earth some two hundred million years ago.

It was the *ALLOSAURUS*, one of the fiercest dinosaurs. The Allosaurus could run very quickly on its powerful hind legs and could balance upright with the aid of its long lizard's tail. It was a meat-eating or carnivorous beast and preyed upon other dinosaurs. Its speed, fierceness and strength made it a threat to even larger creatures, while its claws and teeth were almost invincible weapons. The Allosaurus was one of the first and most dangerous predators.

below: The power crazed Annihilus in conflict with his enemy, the Human Torch.

Annihilus

In the world of Marvel comics, the Negative Zone, a parallel universe existing next to our own, is ruled by the tyrannical, power-crazed *ANNIHILUS*. He began life as a thinking insect, attacked by monsters on a nightmarish planet hidden deep in the heart of the Negative Zone. On an abandoned spaceship he discovered the

Anthropophagai

In his play *Othello*, Shakespeare alludes to:
> 'The *ANTHROPOPHAGI* and men whose heads
> Do grow beneath their shoulders.'

Belief in this race of monstrous men pre-dates Shakespeare by many years. They were supposed to live on a distant island and to have their eyes on their shoulders and their mouths set in their chests. The stories of headless men continued, and were 'confirmed' by early explorers and adventurers, who added an extra note of horror by maintaining that these creatures used human skulls as cups. In 1595 Sir Walter Raleigh published an account of his voyage to Guiana in which he asserted his belief in the Anthropophagi, although he had not had the doubtful pleasure of seeing them for himself. Anthropophagi, incidentally, literally means a cannibal and perhaps such a fearful taste in food caused superstitious people to endow them with an equally horrendous appearance.

Anubis

The Ancient Egyptian monster who decided which hearts Ammit should eat in the underworld Hall of Judgement was named *ANUBIS*. His task was to judge the dead. He had the body of man and the head of a jackal. It was also said that he had devoured his own father.

Argus Panoptes

ARGUS PANOPTES, whose name means 'all-seeing', was so called by the Ancient Greeks because he had a hundred eyes, dispersed all over his body. When the others were closed, two of these eyes always remained open and watchful. He was eventually charmed to sleep by Hermes who then cut off his head. According to legend, the goddess Hera placed his hundred eyes in the peacock's tail as a memorial. For Argus had helped her when she was jealous of her husband Zeus.

above: Antaeus wrestling with the hero Hercules.
opposite: Anubis, the jackal-headed monster.

seeds of life which he has employed for more than a thousand years to increase his own strength and intelligence. Now, in his metallic suit and spiked shoulder pads, with enormous, threatening wings, he plans to take over the world. In order to do this he has declared war on The Fantastic Four, heroic champions of good in the world.

Antaeus

In classical mythology, the son of the sea (Poseidon) and the earth (Gaea) *ANTAEUS* was a giant and a champion wrestler. In fact, he was invincible and killed all his challengers, only to build a macabre house out of their skulls. The secret of his power lay in contact with the earth, his mother. Every time a wrestler threw him down his strength was renewed by the earth. His end came when Hercules discovered this secret and defeated him by raising him into the air and crushing him.

bloodless. The Baobhan Sith usually appear in the form of lovely girls. Their habitual long green dresses are said to hide the fact that they have hooves instead of feet. Other stories maintain that these bloodthirsty creatures appear in the form of ravens and crows.

Banshee

In the folklore of Ireland, the *BANSHEE* is an ugly semi-human spirit who foretells death. She is commonly represented as a washerwoman who spends her life on the banks of a river washing the clothes of someone who is about to die. The Banshee sets up a constant wail and her eyes are horribly red with weeping. She has webbed feet, long straggly hair, a single projecting tooth and only one nostril. If this ugly creature is ever caught by a human being – and it seems unlikely that many people would try to catch her – she must reveal the name of the person who is going to die and grant her captor three wishes. The wail of the Banshee is a ghastly, blood-curdling noise which is still believed to announce the approach of Death.

In Scottish legends, the Banshee is less terrifying; she is a fairy-woman who likes to marry human beings.

Baobhan Sith

An ancient Scottish folk-tale indicates the age and universality of vampire legends. Four hunters in the wilds of Scotland took refuge for the night in an abandoned hut. They began to dance in order to keep warm and to keep their spirits up. One of them wished that their girl friends were there to dance with them. Suddenly, four girls entered the hut. They had long golden hair and wore green dresses. Three of them immediately joined the dance. The fourth sat by the man who had made the wish and who was singing for the others. To his horror, the singer suddenly noticed that his three companions were bleeding as they danced. He knew then that they had encountered the *BAOBHAN SITH*. These are evil, blood-drinking spirits. The singer managed to escape the clutches of his beautiful vampire, but the next morning he found his three companions dead and

below: The Beast from 20,000 Fathoms threatens the city and is undaunted by the armed police.

Basilisk

Many legends about the *BASILISK*, which is also known as the Cockatrice, refer to it as the most deadly of all creatures. It is commonly regarded as the king of serpents because it has a crest or comb on its head and because it can kill all living things except the weasel. Most accounts describe it as a lizard or serpent and all agree that it moved like a snake but with the front part of its body in an upright position. It therefore resembled a walking snake. The Basilisk always lived in deserts because it could kill with a look and its breath withered whatever it touched. Consequently, it created a desert around itself wherever it went. Its deadly properties were such that if a man on horseback tried to kill it with a spear, a poison was believed to travel up the shaft of the weapon and kill both horse and rider.

--WELL, AFTER THIS--WHO'S COUNTING?
I AM THE BI-BEAST! STAND WHERE YOU ARE!
MY SKULL-BROTHER AND I BID YOU WELCOME, STRANGERS.
GOOD LORD!
HUH?

The Basilisk was hatched from a round egg, laid by a cockerel. It had to be hatched by a toad and this could take as long as nine years. Three things only were fatal to the Basilisk: the crow of a cock, the weasel and itself. Legends therefore say that travellers always carried a cock with them on journeys to protect them from the Basilisk. The weasel was the only animal brave enough to attack the Basilisk and was frequently able to kill it, but only at the cost of its own life. The most original way of killing this creature was to use its own powers against it. This could be done very simply, by showing the Basilisk its reflection in a mirror or polished shield, whereupon its own death-bringing stare killed it.

Basilisks and cockatrices are mentioned in the Bible, where they are associated with the Devil, and in Greek and Medieval European legends. As late as the 16th Century, a mirror was still believed to be the best protection against these creatures.

Beast from 20,000 Fathoms

The *BEAST FROM 20,000 FATHOMS* was a giant lizard-like dinosaur, known as a rhedosaur. This gigantic monster was awakened from its million year preservation at the bottom of the sea by an atomic bomb blast. The Beast immediately set about splintering a mountainous iceberg and its adventures, in true movie fashion, eventually led it to New York which it proceeded to demolish.

Bi Beast

BI-BEAST is a creation of the world of Marvel comic monsters. In this infinite universe, of strange and alien creatures, Bi-Beast inhabits a city about eight miles from earth. Created by the bird people, his terrible twinned-skull contains their cultural knowledge and the secrets of their warfare. However the civilization that he guards is slowly dying, due to his lack of scientific knowledge. He is of gargantuan size, with great clawed hands. His enormous strength is of no use, since the machine

left: Bi-Beast guardian of the city in the sky.

which keeps him alive is running down. He discovers that the Hulk is in fact Bruce Banner a scientist and keeps him in the city to maintain the machines. However Bruce Banner is rapidly transformed into the Hulk, and attempts to fight Bi-Beast, but the city is destroyed by Modock.

Blob

Two teenagers saw what they took to be a shooting star fall to earth and set off to find its landing place. En route, they discovered an old man writhing in pain beside the road. His hand was mysteriously covered in some jelly-like substance. They rushed him to hospital and there the doctor discovered that the jelly was spreading all over his body. He was literally turning into the *BLOB*, a sort of enormous jelly fish, or amorphous mass of human-absorbing ectoplasm. First a nurse and then the doctor himself are absorbed into this extra-terrestrial goo. No one, however, will believe the teenagers' story. Meanwhile, the Blob keeps on growing, terrorizing groups of the local citizenry and eventually all but swallowing a mobile cafe and its occupants. Electricity and fire cannot destroy this alien Blob, but the hero – in the then unknown person of Steve McQueen – discovers that it is vulnerable to cold. Once this secret is realised, the Blob is swiftly refrigerated and dumped into the Arctic Ocean where, presumably, it can do no harm. This ending suggests an intention on the part of the makers of the film to thaw the Blob at some future date for a comeback, but this has not yet happened.

Blood beast of Terror

Set in the 1840s the *BLOOD BEAST OF TERROR* concerns a mysterious professor of entomology and his beautiful daughter who have a fondness for conducting strange experiments. Near their house two mysterious deaths occur. Strange petal-like objects are found near the bodies but nobody knows where they came from or what they are. In fact, with the aid of transfusions of blood from other young women, the professor is able to transform his daughter, Clare, into a human-sized Deathshead moth. This moth is a blood-drinking vampire, and soon gets out of hand and when the professor determines to kill it, he too is slaughtered and drained of his blood.

left: Brachiosaurus grazing on the river bed.
right: A battle of strength between an Allosaurus and a Brontosaurus.

Once the existence of the moth-woman is known, the mysterious petals are explained. They are, in fact, scales from her body. The creature is eventually destroyed by being lured to the fire, which moths find irresistible. As the flames consume the Blood Beast, however, its body turns back into that of the young woman, Clare.

Blue Men of the Minch

The strait between the Outer Hebrides and the western coast of Scotland is the home of the *BLUE MEN OF THE MINCH*, as the strait is called. These are a form of evil mermen, coloured blue all over. They are always restless and on the look-out for mischief, and are thus believed to cause storms. Sometimes they actually attack

ships passing through the Minch and try to wreck them. They can be argued with however, and it is believed that the captain of a ship can always out-talk them. He can do this more easily if he can speak to them in rhyme, for this confuses the Blue Men. When they are asleep, it is said, the weather is sure to be fine and the sea calm.

Brachiosaurus

It is generally believed that the *BRACHIO-SAURUS* was the largest of all dinosaurs, weighing almost fifty tons. This great weight made it extremely difficult for him to move, and certainly he could do so only very slowly. Unlike many dinosaurs, the Brachiosaurus used all four legs to get around, but his survival really depended on his very long, straight neck. With the aid of this, he was able to live in deep water which protected him from predators. His nostrils were situated in a sort of dome on the top of his head, so that the whole of his body and face could be submerged in water. Although the Brachiosaurus spent a lot of time in the water for safety reasons, he never learnt to swim. As a result he must have led a very stationary life, grazing on plants which he found on the water bed.

Brontosaurus

The skeleton of a *BRONTOSAURUS* was discovered which, when it was pieced together, was over seventy feet long. This gigantic creature moved on four thick legs and had a very long neck and tail. Indeed, these appendages account for the greater part of its length. Most surprising of all is the minute size of this giant's head. It was no thicker than its neck. This meant that the Brontosaurus had an extremely small brain and had to spend the majority of its time eating in order to sustain such a large body. Its great weight and size made it extremely vulnerable and, like the Brachiosaurus, it sought the protection of water. The long neck of this otherwise cumbersome beast made it possible for it to wade far out into deep water and so avoid its enemies.

Captive Wild Woman

The ever popular theme of man into beast via copious injections of serum was presented in reverse in a film with the self-explanatory title *CAPTIVE WILD WOMAN*. The demented doctor in this case treated a female orang-outang with blood transfusions and glandular extractions taken from a young woman patient. As a result, Cheela the orang-outang became an attractive woman in her own right. The Captive Wild Woman then went to work for a circus and fell in love with its owner. Her animal instincts, however, were still present and prompted her to attack her rival for the circus owner's affections.

Soon she began to revert to her original form, becoming an ugly, hairy lady who had to be rushed back to the sanatorium for further human-making injections. She was released, however, by her rival and immediately dispatched the doctor. Next she rescued the man she loved from the stampeding circus animals, only to be shot by an observer who thought that the hybrid monkey-woman was attacking the circus owner.

below: *The Captive Wild Woman is beautiful.*
bottom: *As an ape the Wild Woman is caged.*

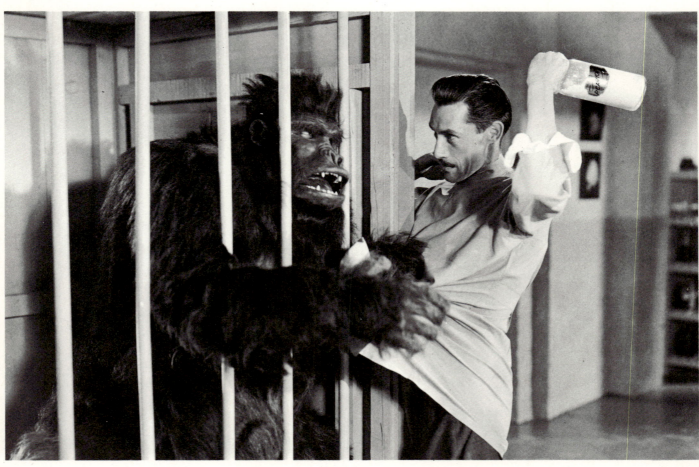

above: Cerberus, the three headed monster-dog.

Centaurs

The *CENTAURS* were monsters only in their physical shape, for their intentions were benevolent. They were a combination of man and horse and were highly regarded for their wisdom and skills. Chiron, the most famous of the Centaurs, was placed among the stars by Zeus and is represented by the constellation Sagittarius.

Cerberus

The job of *CERBERUS* was to guard the gates of Hades which he did by devouring any living creatures who attempted to enter or any shade that tried to leave. This was comparatively easy for him since he was a gigantic dog, with three heads and a stinging serpentine tail. To make him even more vicious and horrible, he had a mane of snakes which would sting anyone who touched him. Even so, three Greek heroes managed to evade him at different times and Hercules succeeded in choking him into submission, despite the bites of his living, reptilian mane, and brought him up from the Underworld into the light of day. This so terrified Cerberus that he began to foam at the mouth and every drop of his saliva that fell to the earth made a poisonous aconite grow.

Belief in Cerberus was so great at one time that the Greeks always buried a small honey cake along with their dead which was said to please and pacify the monstrous watchdog of Hades.

15

Cetus

A ravaging sea monster was created by the Classical gods to punish Cassiopeia for her vanity when she said that she and her daughter were more beautiful than Venus. It demanded her daughter Andromeda in return for a promise to cease its terrorizing. This creature was called *CETUS* and looked like a dolphin with a forked tale but with the head of a greyhound. It would have eaten Andromeda, who was tied to a rock for the monster as the Gods demanded, had it not been defeated by the hero Perseus. In one legend, Cetus was turned to stone by *Medusa's* decapitated head. Cetus is now the name of a constellation of stars which gazes from a distance at Andromeda.

Chichevache

A really unusual monster was the *CHICHEVACHE* whose history demonstrates how legends and myths can illustrate very human ideas. The name Chichevache is a Middle English word and is a corruption of the French *chicheface*, which literally means 'thin face'. The French word *vache* means 'cow'. The monster, therefore, was supposed to be a perpetually thin cow with a human face who fed only on obedient and faithful wives. It was said that there were so few of these to be found that the poor creature was doomed to be forever hungry and undernourished. The Chichevache, despite the French origins of its name, appears to be found only in English lore.

Chimera

One of the many monster-children of Echidna and Typhon in classical mythology, the *CHIMERA* was made up of three parts: the head and front of a lion, the body of a goat and the hindquarters of a dragon. It was sometimes depicted as three-headed, each part of its composite body having its own distinctive head. It was fire-breathing and so was able to destroy anything that came near it. It was eventually killed by the hero Bellerophon, riding the winged horse

left: The Centaurs, half-horse, half-man.
below: The chimera, multi-hybrid monster.

Pegasus which enabled him to evade the beast's fiery breath. The monster's name is today used to describe an unfounded illusion or false hope which perhaps indicates that this particular monster was always a bit far-fetched!

Coelacanth

The fossilised remains of large, ugly fish dating back some sixty or seventy million years were familiar to experts who believed the creature to be extinct, when in 1938, a living specimen was caught off the coast of South Africa. This was the famous 'prehistoric fish', the COELACANTH. That specimen was five feet long and weighed a hundred and twenty-seven pounds. Its luminous dark blue colouring and unusually rough scales indicated that it normally inhabited the very depths of the ocean. In 1952 a second Coelacanth was caught off Madagascar and since then another six have been brought to the surface. These creatures have been caught at a depth of one thousand two hundred feet. They are carnivorous and, more than any other evidence we have, indicate the possibility of unknown or supposedly extinct creatures having survived in the uncharted regions of the seas.

Crab Monsters

Many science fiction films have featured well-known earth dwelling creatures who grow to gargantuan size. The Attack of the CRAB MONSTERS is a notable example. The crabs inhabited an island in the Pacific which became infected by radio-active fallout. This caused the crabs to grow to an enormous size. They quickly developed a taste for human flesh and every time they devoured someone, they mysteriously absorbed his or her memories, mental facilities and voice. The Crab Monsters were eventually blown up and so destroyed.

Creature from the Black Lagoon

An archaeologist working in the depths of the Amazon Jungle discovers a large, fossilised skeleton hand, which has unusual web-fingers. It is thought to date from the Devonian age and on the strength of this discovery, a scientific party is formed to unearth the rest of the skeleton. The search takes the party deeper into the jungle, to a place shrouded in local legend, known as the Black Lagoon. Exploring underwater, the team soon encounter the CREATURE FROM THE BLACK LAGOON.

The Creature, who is also known as the Gill-Man, is a large amphibious man-fish. His scaley body is human in form, but the webbed feet and fingers, together with the gilled fish-head betray his aquatic origins.

Like so many other movie monsters, the Creature is deeply attracted to the one female member of the party. By using an Indian drug sprinkled on the water, the party manage to capture the Gill-Man, but he escapes. They follow him to a vast cavern where he makes his first attempt to capture the girl. Later, after he has killed several of the male members of the team, the Creature builds a dam across the entrance to the lagoon, thus preventing their ship from leaving. While they are trying to unblock the channel, the Creature seizes the girl and carries her off. Only when he is cornered and riddled with bullets do they succeed in rescuing her. The Creature lumbers into the water and is last seen, mortally wounded, floating in his preferred element.

The first Creature film was made in 1954 and contains some spectacular underwater photography. In successive years he reappeared in *Revenge of the Creature* and *The Creature*

left: The unbelievably real Coelacanth.
right: The Creature from the Black Lagoon.

Walks Among Us. In this latter film he was operated on to make him more human, but at the end this amphibious, ugly monster returned again to the watery deeps.

Cybermen

One reason for the continued success of the British TV series *Dr Who* is undoubtedly that it has provided viewers with some new and very interesting monsters. Although the Daleks remain supreme enemies of the Doctor and his companions, he has also had to contend with the awful *CYBERMEN*. These are plastic, robot-like creatures from the planet Telos. In an attempt to make themselves immune to disease and other dangers, they have gradually replaced their ordinary, vulnerable bodies with plastic limbs and features until they are now virtually machines. At the same time they have excluded emotion entirely from their thinking. They operate on pure, implacable logic which makes them totally ruthless. The Cybermen are the invention of two men, Gerry Davis and Kit Pedler, and they first appeared to do battle with Dr Who in 1967. They can be destroyed, fortunately, by laser guns.

Cyclops

These immensely strong giants, distinguished by the fact that they only possessed one terrible eye which was set in the middle of their foreheads, were known as the *CYCLOPS*. They play a varied role in Greek mythology, but are best remembered for the encounter between Ulysses and the most terrible of them all, Polyphemus. Ulysses and a band of sailors came to the island of the Cyclops in search of provisions and entered Polyphemus' cave. He ate two sailors for

left: The giant Cyclops with his one-eyed stare.
below: The Cybermen, from Dr. Who.

supper and another two for breakfast. When he left the cave with his herd of sheep, he rolled a gigantic boulder in front of it which twenty oxen could not move.

On the second night, Ulysses made Polyphemus drunk with a jar of wine he had brought to barter for food. Then he blinded the Cyclops with his own staff, the point of which Ulysses and his men hardened in the fire. They then escaped from the cave by clinging to the underbellies of Polyphemus' sheep so that although he felt each sheep as it passed he did not discover them. In his rage, Polyphemus called for help from the other one-eyed giants but when he told them that he had been blinded by Noman – the name Ulysses had given himself – they assumed his blindness was a punishment from the gods and would not help him. Just before boarding his ship, Ulysses revealed his true identity, whereupon the Cyclops tore up a vast rock and hurled it into the sea, nearly swamping the ship.

Cyclops is also the name of a favourite Marvel comic-character. He is the command leader of the mutant X men and his real identity is Scott Walker. Unlike the original Cyclops, he has both eyes, but they are able to emit an optical beam. Because of this his eyes are always covered, with dark glasses in his ordinary life, and by a slit-like vizor when he is in his special Cyclops uniform. This, of course, gives him a one-eyed appearance, hence his name.

Cyoeraeth

Many of the monstrous creatures of folk-lore have as their specific function the announcement of impending death. An old Welsh legend tells of a fearful moaning shriek heard only at night and only at crossroads or near a river. When the cry is heard at the river it is invariably accompanied by the splashing of water, as though the creature who makes this unearthly howl is trying to give as much warning as possible. The source of the cry seldom made itself visible to men. When it did, however, it appeared and dressed as a woman, with wild, tangled hair and long, withered arms. Its face was described as bloodless and ghastly and it had long, black teeth. The name of this spirit was CYOERAETH.

right: The black and white Daleks from Dr. Who.

Daleks

Nobody can say for certain when a terrible neutron war broke out on the distant planet of Skara. What is known is that the inhabitants were severely affected by radiation. In fact, they were reduced to bodiless brains, deprived even of their voices. In order to move around they had to invent a metallic case, complete with electronic voice box. These travelling containers, which also have mechanical grab-like arms and a single electronic eye, house the *DALEKS*, the implacable enemies of Dr Who in the British TV series. The Daleks were invented by a television script-writer called Terry Nation and first appeared in the second adventure of *Dr Who*. They became an immediate success and are now one of the most popular monster races in the world. Perhaps because of the tragic loss of their own bodies, the Daleks seem to hate everything. No doubt their repeated attempts to take over the universe will

continue to exercise Dr Who's ingenuity for many years to come.

above: *Dr. Who, with two of his old enemies, the Daleks, in episode one of 'Planet of the Daleks'.*

Dark Messiah

A fairly recent addition to the galaxy of arch-enemies sent to plague the super-heroes of comic-land is the *DARK MESSIAH*. This purple-clad, muscular cross between a tyrant and a hot-gospeller was once a harmless gymnast called Mordecai Jones. While performing acrobatic feats in the street one day, he was attacked by a dog which caused him to fall on his head and lose consciousness. He was overlooked in the busy emergency department of the local hospital and kidnapped by a hooded stranger who wired his unconscious body to a sinister machine. Thus Mordecai Jones was translated into the Dark Messiah, complete with eyes that can project a weird purple beam which demolishes walls and anything else that gets in his way. The Dark Messiah is being used as a pawn in some master-plan, but his power and mysteriously acquired attributes make him an extremely formidable enemy.

Devils

DEVILS is the collective name for evil spirits who have been lost to *SATAN*.

SATAN is the prince of darkness, the King of all evil. He was once Lucifer, the brightest and most beautiful angel of them all, who was cast out of Heaven because he claimed to be as great as God, thus committing the Sin of Pride. God did not destroy Lucifer, but condemned him instead to the pits and fires of Hell for all eternity. He is said to enjoy the innocent blood of sacrificial victims

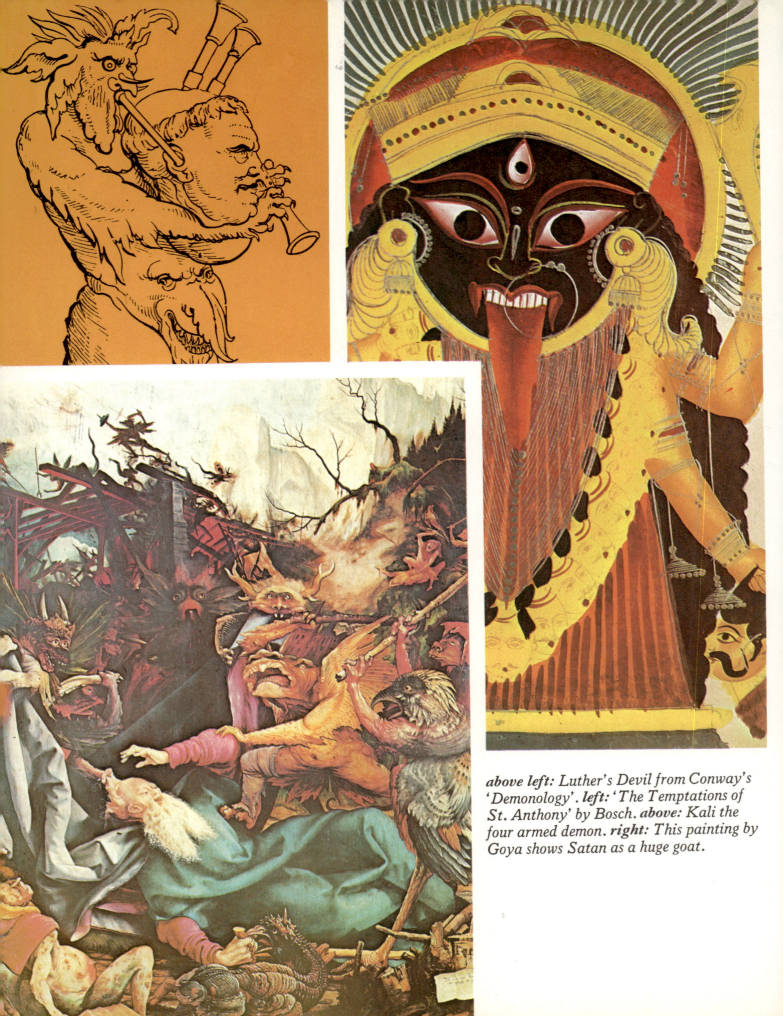

above left: Luther's Devil from Conway's 'Demonology'. *left:* 'The Temptations of St. Anthony' by Bosch. *above:* Kali the four armed demon. *right:* This painting by Goya shows Satan as a huge goat.

which his followers offer him, notably that of young virgins and innocent babes. He is able to assume any form but is usually depicted with the head of a goat.

The demons serve their master in luring the souls of the living to damnation. In order to do this they promise great wealth, political power, or eternal youth or beauty. They frequently appear as horned men with forked tails, or in hybrid form. But like Satan they can assume any shape.

Dracae

English water spirits are traditionally known as *DRACAE*. They are shape-changers who, according to legend, are to be seen floating down the river in the form of wooden dishes. By this device, they tempt women to try to recover the dishes. The moment an unsuspecting woman does this, the Dracae change to their normal human shape and drag her down to the river bed. These captured human women are then required to nurse the Dracae children.

Dracula

From the grim battlements of a sinister half-ruined castle a large black bat glides silently in search of a victim. The bat is Count *DRACULA*, lord of the vampires, lusting for the blood of innocent peasants and unwary travellers in his Transylvanian homeland. We all know this picture of the monster Dracula, star of dozens of films, and his popularity is growing. But where does the legend of Dracula originate?

'His face was a strong – a very strong – aquiline, with high bridge of the thin nose and peculiarly arched nostrils . . . His eyebrows were very massive, almost meeting over the nose, and with bushy hair that seemed to curl in its own profusion. The mouth, so far as I could see it under the heavy moustache, was fixed and rather cruel-looking, with peculiarly sharp white teeth . . . For the rest his ears were pale and at the tops extremely pointed; the chin was broad and strong, and the cheeks firm though thin. The general effect was one of extraordinary pallor.'

This is how Bram Stoker describes Dracula in the famous novel which launched one of the most evil of all monsters on an unsuspecting world. Bram Stoker was born in Ireland in 1847 and had a varied and energetic career. At one time he was a civil servant, but the most important phase of his career was spent as business manager to the great English actor, Henry Irving. This was an arduous job, but somehow Stoker found time to write a string of books including romances, thrillers and some for children. *Dracula*, by many regarded as the peak of English horror stories, was published in 1897. Sadly, Bram Stoker died in 1912, before the full success of his book and the extent of its influence could be seen.

His novel is long and involved, but full of atmosphere and startling incident. It begins with the journal of a young Englishman, Jonathan Harker, who is travelling to Dracula's castle in Transylvania in order to finalize the purchase by the Count of an English estate. Harker knows that 'every superstition in the world is gathered into the horseshoe of the Carpathians' and as he draws closer to his destination so he becomes aware of the terror people fear at the very mention of the name Dracula.

After a nightmare journey, pursued by wolves, Harker finds himself a virtual prisoner in the gaunt, half-ruined castle and soon discovers a number of hair-raising facts about his host. He casts no reflection in a mirror and only appears at night. He has the habit of crawling like a lizard down the sheer walls of his ghostly castle and returns from these trips with live children which he feeds to three beautiful vampire girls, who are also promised that they can drink Harker's blood when he has served Dracula's purpose. Replete with blood, Dracula sleeps in a coffin during the day. To make matters worse, the Count is visibly growing younger.

left: Dracula in flight in 'Brides of Dracula'.
right top: Christopher Lee as Count Dracula in action.
right below: Is this the end of Dracula at last?

After he has managed to escape from the castle and has recovered from his ordeal, Harker marries his English fiancee Mina. Dracula, however, tries to make Mina Harker his slave by drinking her blood and forcing her to drink his. Before sinking his fangs into her throat he says: 'First a little refreshment to reward my exertions.'

'Kneeling on the near edge of the bed facing outwards was the white clad figure of his (Jonathan Harker's) wife. By her side stood a tall, thin man, clad in black. His face was turned from us, but the instant we saw it we all recognised the Count – in every way, even to the scar on his forehead. With his left hand he held both Mrs Harker's hands, keeping them away with her arms at full tension; his right hand gripped her by the back of the neck, forcing her face down on his bosom. Her white nightdress was smeared with blood, and a thin stream trickled down the man's bare breast, which was shown by his torn-open dress. The attitude of the two had a terrible resemblance to a child forcing a kitten's nose into a saucer of milk to compel it to drink. As we burst into the room, the Count turned his face, and the hellish look that I had heard described seemed to leap into it. His eyes flamed red with devilish passion; the great nostrils of the white aquiline nose opened wide and quivered at the edges; and the white sharp teeth, behind the full lips of the blood-dripping mouth, champed together like those of a wild beast.'

Mina Harker's partial enslavement enables Van Helsing and the others to follow Dracula back to Transylvania where he is destroyed. His throat is cut and he is pierced through the heart, whereupon his body crumbles away to dust.

Bram Stoker muddled together a lot of lore about vampires and added various colourful touches of his own. Dracula is a shape-changer, who appears as a wolf and a bat. Some legends regard werewolves, incidentally, as an intermediary stage on the journey from human being to un-dead vampire. It is entirely Stoker's invention that Dracula can appear as a mist, creeping into rooms, and as a cloud of dust dancing in a mysterious beam of light. On the other hand, the freshness of the un-dead corpses, the plentiful use of garlic as a protection against these creatures and the method of killing them are all taken directly from East European vampire legends.

Stoker must have done quite a lot of background research for his book and he mixed historical fact into his fiction in a most persuasive way. His Dracula, for example, is said to be centuries old. That part of Hungary which he inhabits was for centuries the scene of fierce battles and almost ceaseless war. Dracula is said to have been present at many of these and to be nurtured by the blood-drenched soil of his native land. He is an aristocrat, who despises the peasants and rejoices in the war-like deeds of the noble people he represents. This mixture of history, fiction and folklore leads us to the question, 'Was there ever such a man as Dracula?' Research has shown that there probably was.

Even today in the Carpathian mountains stories are told of one Vlad Dracula, more commonly known as Vlad the Impaler. Since quite a lot is known about this fifteenth century tyrant, and since Bram Stoker obviously borrowed his name, it is fair to assume that his research for *Dracula* brought him into contact with documents concerning the real-life ruler. Indeed, contemporary woodcuts used to illustrate pamphlets about Vlad bear a resemblance to the fiendish Count Dracula described by Stoker in his book.

Vlad the Impaler was a severe and autocratic ruler who got his nickname from his habit of having people impaled on great wooden stakes. He was feared and openly criticized – at one time he was thrown into jail for his misdeeds – but many of the local stories about him say that though he was harsh, he was also just. His slaughtering and tortures were not, it is said, perpetrated out of mindless cruelty but as part of an attempt to make a better society for his people. Be that as it may, his fondness for impaling people – once he is said to have sat down to breakfast in the middle of a forest of impaled and writhing bodies – and his habit of making some of his victims eat each other's cooked flesh, have obvious links with the fictional Dracula. Furthermore, several stories are told of Vlad Dracula having the hats of people who offended him nailed to their heads.

Whether the practice of driving nails through the heads of vampires derives from these incidents or *vice-versa* is one of the mysteries of legend. Certainly there is no scrap of evidence to suggest that Vlad the Impaler was a vampire, but so many of his actions have links with vampire legends that it seems that Bram Stoker exploited this connection in his book.

opposite top: Bram's Castle, Roumania, the birthplace of Dracula. opposite: Dracula's Castle.

For most of us, Dracula's popularity stems from the cinema and means the character interpreted by Bela Lugosi, the aptly Hungarian-born actor who will always be remembered as the blood-thirsty count. Stoker's novel was first filmed in Germany in 1922, however, under the title *Nosferatu*, which is a German name for the un-dead and vampires. This Dracula was gaunt and bald, with madly staring eyes and enormous claws on the ends of his fingers. Bela Lugosi originally played Dracula on the stage and his film version of 1930 established both him and Dracula as stars. Since then the film industry has constantly revived the evil count, and has given him sons and daughters returning from the grave to carry on the family blood-drinking business. Like Franken-stein's monster, Dracula seems to be permanently un-dead, no matter how often he is exorcised with crosses and despite a ton of timber being driven through his celluloid heart.

Of all the popular monster legends, that of Dracula is, in many ways, the most believable. It touches on very real human fears – of ghosts and the loss of life-blood – and uses symbols, like bats, which are familiar and generally held to be unpleasant. Above all, nearly every part of his elaborate story contains a grain of truth, of possi-bility, and that is what makes Dracula both terrifying and irresistible.

Dragons

DRAGONS are universal although their form and habits vary from one land to another. The Dragon of Wantley, described in an old ballad, is fairly typical of the European species.

> *This dragon had two furious wings,*
> *Each one upon each shoulder;*
> *With a sting in his tayl, as long as a flayl,*
> *Which made him bolder and bolder.*
> *He had long claws, and in his jaws*
> *Four-and-forty teeth of iron;*
> *With a hide as tough as any buff,*
> *Which did him round environ.*

Of all the mythological beasts, the dragon, in its Western form at least, most closely resembles the dinosaurs, although it is often said to be made up of portions of many different animals.

The earliest stories about dragons said that they lived at the bottom of the sea where they jealously guarded great hordes of pearls. Later, dragons were described as mainly serpentine, with the

wings and feet of an eagle, fish-like scales, horns and the head of a lion. They are sometimes green, sometimes red, as in the Welsh Dragon, sometimes black and occasionally yellow or white. The one thing all dragons have in common is their ability to breathe out smoke and fire. Their eyes, too, are usually red and fiery. In Africa, the Dragon is believed to be the offspring of an eagle and a wolf. Because this is an unnatural union the Dragon is regarded as totally evil.

The dragon is supposed to fear only one creature, the elephant, which it is able to kill but the elephant crushes it as it falls. Many legends state that eating the blood or heart and liver of the dragon enables men to understand the language of animals. Some stories suggest that dead men are changed into dragons, while their more popular association with death is as fierce guardians of treasure-filled tombs. A common belief is that if

the teeth of a dragon are planted in the earth they will magically grow into an army of men.

The Dragon of Wantley lived off herds of cattle and the occasional child, but a favourite dragon-food appears to have been young virgins. It was to protect one poor girl from a voracious dragon that St George fought his famous battle. Many other saints also slew dragons which had come to represent the power of evil, and from these legends came the romantic, chivalric idea of the knights who were forever rescuing fair, distressed damsels from the greedy jaws of hungry dragons.

Not all dragons, however, were human-eating monsters. The most important of the more friendly kind is the benevolent Chinese Dragon. This beast is an extraordinary mixture, according to one Chinese authority, of camel, clam, tiger, snake, carp, eagle and bull, with a heavily bewhiskered face. The Chinese Dragon was believed to control the four elements and the destiny of man. He was particularly fond of swallows and was said to be jealous of any human being who had eaten this particular bird.

The most popular image of the dragon today is that found in heraldry. This creature is virtually armour-plated with scales and has a row of spines extending along his back. He has clawed feet and the wings of a very large bat. The heraldic dragon is actually a symbol of power but because the majority of people learn about the terrible fire-belching, virgin-eating dragons of myth and fairy tale, he is still chiefly regarded as a malevolent, bad-tempered monster living in a cave, surrounded by the bones of his victims.

below: '*The dragon has two furious wings,*
Each one upon each shoulder'.

Echidna

Although she is not particularly well-known in her own right, *ECHIDNA* was the mother of many of the most famous monsters in Greek mythology. She had the upper body and head of a beautiful woman, but below the waist she was a monstrous serpent. With her husband Typhon she bred Cerberus and Orthos, the Hydra, the Chimera, Ladon and the Sphinx. Some stories claim that this latter monster was actually the progeny of Echidna and her own two-headed son, Orthos.

below: '*Orestes pursued by the furies*', *by C. Rolt.*

Echidna lived in a foul cave and was slain by Argus, the many-eyed.

Elasmosaurus

Some species of dinosaur-like creatures lived in the sea. One of the largest of these was the *ELASMOSAURUS*, a sort of sea-serpent which grew to a length of fifty feet. These creatures had very long tails and necks and propelled themselves through the water with the aid of four large fins or flippers. They had very sharp teeth and lived on fish. They must have been able to move very swiftly, making them a very formidable enemy of other sea-dwelling creatures.

Empusae

Cannibalistic female monsters known as *EMPUSAE* have often been confused with the Lamiae in Classical mythology. They were half-ass and half-human, but could change themselves into bitches, cows or beautiful maidens. In these

above: Echidna the mother of many monsters shown here with her children and husband.

shapes they lured and devoured travellers. In some variations of their history they are blood-sucking, vampire-like creatures.

Erichthonius

Originally, according to the legends of the ancient Greeks, the crow was white in colour. How it came to be changed to black is told in the story of *ERICHTHONIUS*. This monster-child was the product of Hephaestus and the earth goddess Gaea. He was half-human and half-serpent. He was abandoned by his mother and taken up by another goddess, Athena. She placed the ugly baby in a chest and entrusted this to the care of three princesses, the daughters of the King of Athens. They were told never to open the chest but of course, their curiosity got the better of them. When they opened it and saw the half serpentine child they became mad with terror, and threw themselves off the Acropolis. Athena was so sad when she heard of their deaths that she changed the colour of the crow, who had brought her the news, to black as a sign of perpetual mourning. After this she reared Erichthonius herself, and according to some stories, she gave him the power to restore life by giving him some drops of Medusa's blood. Later, despite his monstrous body, Erichthonius became King of Athens.

Erinnyes

Tisiphone, Megara and Alecto were the individual names of three infernal goddesses whose task it was to punish any crime committed within the family. Collectively they were known in Greek Mythology as the *ERINNYES* and they were particularly concerned with avenging the victims of patricide. When they heard of such a crime they immediately appeared outside the house of the guilty person and took up guard. Their hair bristled with hissing serpents and they carried whips and flaming torches. It was impossible for anyone to escape them, for they would pursue the guilty even in the underworld. There was, how-ever, one exception to their policy of revenge. They are said to have shown mercy and leniency to Orestes, who killed his mother. This was because his crime was committed to avenge his father, Agamemnon, who had been slain by his wife. In this connection they became known as the Eumenides, or Benevolent Ones.

Fachen

An Irish legend tells of an awful monster that pursued, mutilated and killed travellers by night. Its body was covered with feathers, a tuft of which stuck up like a cock's comb on its horrible head. A single, gnarled hand grew out of its feathery chest, and one leg grew out of its body at an angle. To make it even more terrifying the *FACHAN* as it was called, had only one eye set in the middle of its forehead. To appear even more menacing, it would ruffle up its ghastly feathers before striking its victim.

Fafner and Fasolt

The legendary giant *FAFNER* and his equally evil brother *FASOLT* are probably most familiar today as characters in Richard Wagner's opera cycle *The Ring of the Nibelungs*. In the original myth dating from the Dark Ages, these brothers killed their father in order to obtain his golden treasure. In the operatic version, Fafner kills Fasolt and, as in the original story, changes himself into a hideous dragon in order to guard the gold. When the hero Siegfried has killed Fafner, his blood enables Siegfried to understand what the birds are saying.

Fantastic Four

The *FANTASTIC FOUR* are among the most popular superheroes in Marvel comics. All four are the victims of gamma rays, to which they were exposed during a space flight in a rocket built by their leader, Reed Richards, who is the world's leading scientist. Richards is now known as *MR FANTASTIC* and has the ability to make his body stretch over a hundred yards. His arch-enemy is Dr Doom against whom he frequently battles with his comrades the Human Torch,

Invisible Girl and the Thing. Lately many of their adventures have involved Medusa rather than Invisible Girl.

Fly

A composite monster – a sort of science-fiction version of the fabulous beasts of folk-lore and legend – was created in a film called *THE FLY* (1958). The story concerned a scientist who invented a means of transmitting matter from one place to another. Unfortunately for him, he failed to notice, when he got into the machine, that a fly was sharing it with him. As a result, when the machine reassembled the man and the fly, they both became monstrous hybrids. The scientist had the much enlarged head and one arm of the fly, while its missing parts were replaced by a miniature human head and arm.

Both of these mixed-up creatures met horrible fates. The scientist's ugly head was crushed in a hydraulic press, while the semi-human fly was helplessly trapped in a spider's web. The idea was revamped in subsequent films, but *The Fly* remains the most successful and the most terrifying.

Frankenstein

One of the most popular and durable monsters of all time has no name of his own and was invented by a young woman of twenty, during a wet summer holiday. Mary Shelley, was the wife of the poet, Percy Bysshe Shelley who took her to Switzerland in the summer of 1816. The bad weather kept the Shelleys and their friend, Lord Byron, indoors a great deal and they amused themselves by reading a French translation of some German ghost stories. This gave them the idea, originally proposed by Lord Byron, that they should each write a ghost story of their own. Mary Shelley was the only member of the group to finish her tale which, after various revisions and additions, was published in 1818 under the title *FRANKENSTEIN*.

The book was an immediate success and is today regarded as a masterpiece of gothic horror.

opposite: The Fantastic Four, a portrait of the Super-heroes from the mighty world of Marvel.

THE MIGHTY WORLD OF MARVEL
PIN-UP PAGE!
THE FANTASTIC FOUR
THE GREATEST TEAM OF SUPER-HEROES THE WORLD HAS EVER KNOWN!
4
Sincerely, Ben, Reed, Sue, & Johnny

Present-day readers who are more familiar with the many subsequent film versions and elaborations of the story are more likely to be struck by the high moral tone of the original than by its horrific content. Mary Shelley was more concerned to write an allegory about man's responsibility and inhumanity than to provide suspense and chills. However, the idea through which she expressed this allegory is so original and exciting that it has fascinated readers, film-makers and audiences for over a hundred and fifty years. For this reason alone, the original is worthy of consideration.

In common with many Victorian novels, Frankenstein's story is told in a most complicated fashion. A young Englishman who has set out to explore the Arctic seas encounters Victor Frankenstein adrift on an ice-floe and takes him aboard his ship. Frankenstein tells him how he had become interested in science and, without giving any details, how he had made a monstrous human being. Mary Shelley's description of this moment is interesting, not least because it shows how greatly the monster has changed over the years.

'It was already one in the morning; the rain pattered dismally against the panes, and my candle was nearly burnt out, when by the glimmer of the half-extinguished light, I saw the dull yellow eye of the creature open; it breathed hard and a convulsive motion agitated its limbs.

'How can I describe my emotions at this catastrophe, or how delineate the wretch whom with such infinite pains and care I had endeavoured to form? His limbs were in proportion, and I had selected his features as beautiful. Beautiful! Great God! His yellow skin scarcely covered the work of muscles and arteries beneath; his hair was of a lustrous black, and flowing; his teeth of pearly whiteness; but these luxuriances only formed a more horrid contrast with his watery eyes, that seemed almost of the same colour as the dun white sockets in which they were set, his shrivelled complexion and straight black lips.'

Frankenstein immediately fled in terror from his monster who disappeared. In fact, the monster made his way to Switzerland, where Frankenstein lived, and murdered his younger

left: The monster lives again in the 20th. Century-Fox production 'The Return of the Fly.'

brother. Frankenstein knew that the monster was responsible but dared not tell anyone because he knew that he would not be believed. As a result of his silence, a young servant girl is executed for his brother's murder.

Frankenstein later encounters the monster in the mountains and learns how he has survived and suffered. The monster is essentially loving and kindly, but he is driven to desperate acts by his loneliness and the hatred he inspires in mankind. He promises Frankenstein that he will never harm another living soul if his creator will make him a female companion to dispel his loneliness.

'I am alone and miserable,' the monster says. 'Man will not associate with me; but one as deformed and horrible as myself would not deny herself to me. My companion must be of the same species, and have the same defects. This being you must create.'

Frankenstein agrees and, after much delay, travels to the Orkney islands and begins work on the second monster. He realizes, however, that these two creatures might breed and that the female he is about to create might not share the original monster's determination not to harm people. He therefore destroys the second monster, only to receive this terrible curse from the mouth of the lonely original: 'I will be with you on your wedding night.'

First however, the monster murders Frankenstein's best friend and for a time Frankenstein is suspected of the murder. When Frankenstein is freed from jail, he marries Elizabeth who is strangled by the monster on their wedding night. Thereafter, Frankenstein devotes his life to the pursuit of the monster whom he has vowed to destroy. He has pursued him across Russia and on to the Arctic wastes where the original narrator of the story, Robert Walton, has found him. Soon after completing his tale, Frankenstein dies and the monster boards the ship to mourn the loss of his creator and to repent the evil he has committed. Saying that he is soon to die, the monster leaps out of the cabin window and disappears into the icy wastes.

The original *Frankenstein* has never been faithfully adapted to the screen probably because of the difficulties in translating Mary Shelley's central argument into visual terms. The first film version, made in 1910, was in fact adapted from a play and although the actor who portrayed the monster, Charles Ogle, is said to have modelled his make-up on Mary Shelley's description, this

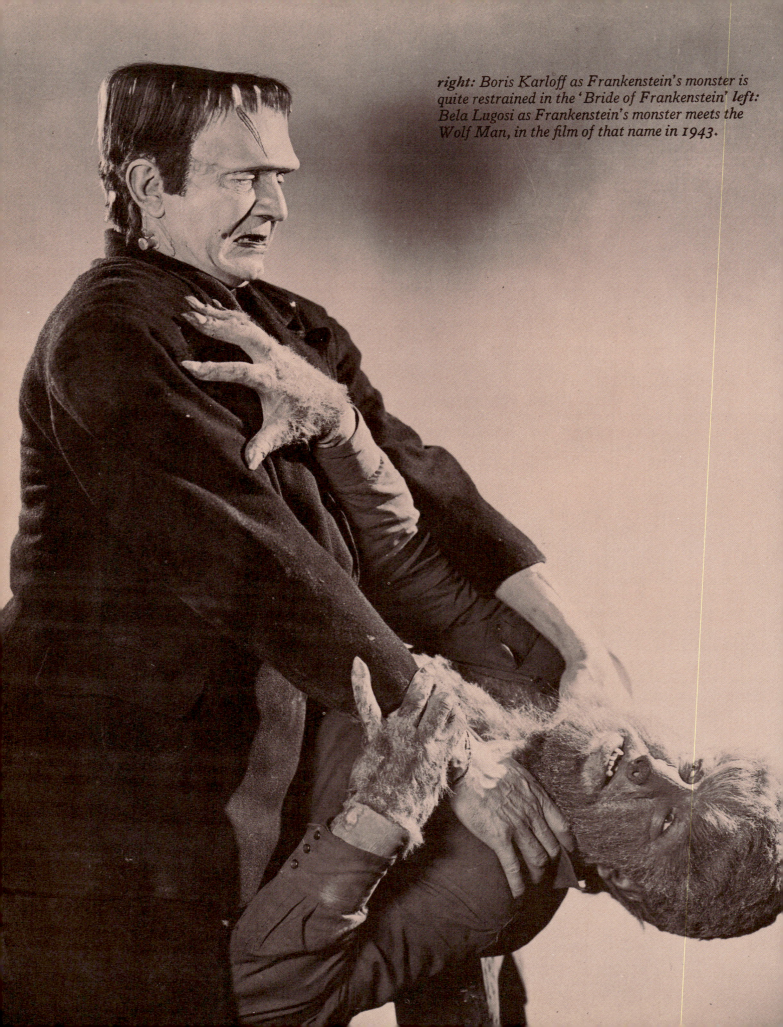

right: Boris Karloff as Frankenstein's monster is quite restrained in the 'Bride of Frankenstein' *left*: Bela Lugosi as Frankenstein's monster meets the Wolf Man, in the film of that name in 1943.

film established the cinema's concern with the horrific rather than the philosophical aspects of the story.

The most influential film, which set the pattern followed by others for over twenty years, was made in 1931 and was also simply called *Frankenstein*. This made three important changes to the original novel. Frankenstein himself became a baron. His elevation to the aristocracy is thought to have been dictated by the box-office since the film followed a successful version of Dracula, who was, of course, a Count. More significantly, the monster was accidentally given a criminal brain which is an idea far removed from Mary Shelley's original conception. She had been concerned to show how bad treatment and loneliness brought out the criminal side of the monster's essentially human nature. This change, however, enabled the film to stress the horrific elements in the story. The most important contribution of all was the casting of Boris Karloff as the monster and the invention of a make-up for him which provided the world with a recognisable image of the monster.

This make-up took three and a half hours to put on and exaggerated Karloff's own features. The Karloff monster looks as though he has been stitched together by a very inexpert craftsman indeed. He has a deathly, sewn-together appearance which is almost human, which perhaps plays on our fears of surgery and which certainly established the popular idea of the creature's appearance.

The fact that Mary Shelley left his fate unresolved has enabled film-makers to revive him time and time again. Frankenstein's monster has survived in an underground pool, been preserved in a pit of sulphur, originally intended to destroy him and has been frequently 'frozen' in blocks of ice, in a state of suspended animation.

The popularity of the story is such that Mexican, Spanish and Japanese film versions have been made and, in the late 1950's there was something of a Frankenstein revival. *The Curse of Frankenstein* returned to Mary Shelley's original but was unable, due to copyright difficulties, to reproduce the Karloff make-up. Christopher Lee gave him an appearance which was much closer to Mary Shelley's description. In *The Revenge of Frankenstein*, the evil scientist manufactured a new cannibalistic monster, while in *Frankenstein Created Woman* the soul of a man inhabited the body of a beautiful

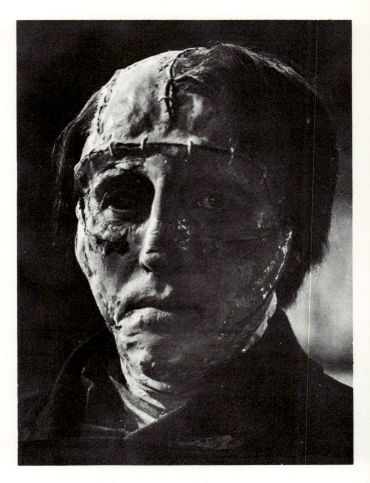

above: Christopher Lee as Frankenstein's monster.

woman who set out to destroy those who had caused her original death.

The real fascination of the Frankenstein story is the idea of a man creating a living creature which becomes his destroyer. This idea, which interested Mary Shelley enormously, can still be found in virtually all versions, even though everything else has been changed. Partly because Mary Shelley never gave her monster a name and partly because of the popularity of Boris Karloff's performance and make-up, the identity of the creator (Frankenstein), and the created have become confused. The name Frankenstein now conjures up a picture of Karloff's half-human form, and the popularity of the monster undoubtedly stems as much from him as from Mrs Shelley.

The famous film publicist's phrase, 'You can't keep a good monster down', was invented to advertise a Frankenstein movie and is entirely apt. No matter what his fate, Frankenstein's monster always rises again to haunt and horrify us.

Gabriel Ratchets

According to an ancient legend peculiar to the North of England, there is a pack of hounds which hunt high up in the sky during thunderstorms. Their cries can be heard mingled with the raging of the storms. They are called *GABRIEL RATCHETS* and their chilling cry is said to announce the approach of death. Some people used to believe that they were the spirits of children who had died without being baptised. Gabriel Ratchets are therefore described as restless souls who hunt for others to join their ghostly pack.

Gamma People

The *GAMMA PEOPLE* are the sad victims of experimental brain surgery, which by the use of gamma rays, is supposed to turn ordinary mortals into geniuses. These experiments are conducted by Boronsky, the dictator of Gudavia, a mythical European state. More often than not the operation

above: '*The Merchant and the Genius*'. *below:* The geni appearing to Aladdin and his mother.

goes wrong, turning the victims into brainless, willess zombies. These dire experiments are uncovered by two newspapermen in a film called *The Gamma People*. The reporters themselves are almost processed by the operation, but succeed in blowing up the evil laboratory in the nick of time. Happily, some of the Gamma People are restored to normality, and all are freed from the evil will of the dictator.

Genii

According to the ancient mythology of Assyria and Babylonia, there were many sorts of *GENII*. Some of these were essentially good, others could be controlled by prayers and offerings, but seven of them were so dangerous and malevolent that nobody could control them – not even the gods themselves. They were spirits who lived in holes in the earth and they made men quarrel, spread diseases and caused all the other troubles that plague mankind. When, rarely, they appeared to human beings, they assumed a terrifying form. Their favourite shape was a human body, with a lion's head, armed with many horns. On their grizzly hands they had powerful, tearing claws. Fortunately, the Genii never married or bred so that at least their number was limited.

Geryon

GERYON was said in classical myth to be the strongest man alive. Since he possessed three bodies, joined at the waist, three heads and six hands, his great strength is easily explained. He had a herd of unique red cattle which Hercules had to steal from him. He managed to kill this triple man by shooting him through the side so that the arrow penetrated all three bodies.

Giants

GIANTS appear in all mythologies and are frequently connected with stories of the creation of the world. Originally giants were simply very large men. Many were kindly and benevolent, while others were represented as being slow and stupid. It is the evil Giant who lives on in fairy-tales and old legends. Many years ago, when belief in these creatures was much more widespread, wicked giants were known by the separate name, Ogres. These were generally defined as hideous, man-eating monsters. Today, at least in common usage, the two words are quite interchangeable.

Greek legends are peopled with highly individual giants. A whole race of them, the Titans,

below: Hercules doing battle with Geryon, the triple bodied man. opposite: 'Thor's fight with the giants,' by Winge, from the Stockholm Gallery.

above: These giant skeleton warriors sprang from the earth where Jason cast the dragon's teeth.

waged war against the gods and they bred the even more horrible Gigantes. All the Gigantes were horrendously ugly. Some had Dragons' tails, some had fifty heads and others were half serpent with a hundred arms. Hercules, with the aid of Zeus, is usually credited with ridding the world of the Gigantes, who were variously clubbed to death or buried under mountains.

The most famous English giants are undoubtedly Gog and Magog. According to legend, the thirty-two daughters of the Emperor Diocletian journeyed to Albion – the ancient name for Britain – and there mated with native devils. The result of this union was a race of giants. Albion was later conquered by the Trojan, Brutus, who divided the land into Britain and Cornwall. This latter kingdom was ruled by one of Brutus' retinue, a giant named Corinaeus. The only surviving member of the giant race, Gogmagog, who was over twelve feet tall and could uproot trees with one hand, fought a battle with Corinaeus. Gogmagog crushed three of Corinaeus' ribs which so enraged the Trojan that he hurled Gogmagog into the sea. It is thought that the British giants' name was later split and that Corineaus became known as Gog.

In other versions, there are always two giants

surviving Brutus' occupation, Gog and Magog. They were captured and taken in chains to London where they were made to work as porters. The statues of Gog and Magog can still be seen in the Guildhall, London.

Many of the most popular and durable stories about giants illustrate the ultimate superiority of brain over brawn. David and Goliath is one of the most familiar examples. Goliath is thought to have been over nine feet tall and to have worn a coat of chain-mail which weighed about two hundred and eight pounds. The giant slain by the intrepid Jack is claimed as a native of many countries, including Wales. In that perenially popular version, the giant was a two-headed monster who ate human beings. His castle was situated in Flintshire. His famous catch-phrase, 'Fe fi fo fum, I smell the blood of an Englishman' is said to have been borrowed from an old Mohammedan story.

Cornwall, perhaps because it was originally ruled by a giant, is rich in giant-lore. King Arthur himself did battle with a giant who made his home on top of St Michael's Mount and carried off beautiful maidens. Arthur climbed to the giant's lair and found him warming himself in front of a great fire and popping whole men into his mouth. Fortunately, Arthur defeated him in the ensuing fight and cut off his head.

Other notable Cornish giants had similar cannibalistic habits. One, fried children daily, on a flat rock in front of his cave and had arms so long that he could snatch sailors from boats passing Land's End. The giant Wrath, on the other hand, used to wade out into the sea and attach ships to his belt. Then he would carry them back to his lair in order to devour the crew and passengers.

Virtually all North American giants are cannibalistic, but they may be in the form of a bird or animal as well as that of a human. One of the most famous is a giant bird which greatly resembles the Roc, even to the extent of carrying a boy to the top of a cliff, in much the same way as Sinbad was carried by the Roc.

The most celebrated of all the Irish giants was Fingal. As a youth he served a long apprenticeship

under another giant and obtained the gift of prophecy by eating the first piece of a salmon. Later in his career, Fingal created the Giant's Causeway which can still be seen in Northern Ireland.

On the whole giants tend to be male, but a particularly unpleasant female of the species, Grana, also lived in Ireland. She was a wizened old woman who lured people to her cave by lighting a candle each night. She was vanquished, but not killed, by a man named Regan who climbed up to her cave and blew out the fatal candle. This so enraged Grana that she snatched up an enormous rock and hurled it after him. This rock is still to be seen and, despite its great size and weight, it is said to carry the impress of Grana's powerful fingers on its surface.

Very old Norse and Teuton legends maintain that the world was created by a god from the body of the first giant. His name was Ymir and a whole race of other giants was born from his sweat. When the god emerged from the ice, he slew Ymir and made the world. Ymir's body became the earth and the seas were made of his blood. His gigantic bones became the mountains, while his skull made the sky. His hair was fashioned into trees, and his brains became the clouds. The place

below: Jason and his men flee across the beach at the sight of the angry giant, sword in hand.

where man dwelt was called Midgard and was made from Ymir's eyebrows. All but two of Ymir's offspring were drowned in his blood when the seas were formed. The survivors, Bergelmir and his wife, fled to the edge of the world and built themselves a remote home. It is believed that all subsequent giants are descended from them.

The idea of the earth being constructed out of a giant's body, or created by a giant dropping stones and boulders as he strode across the world is a familiar one. Most mythologies have some version of this creation story. For the most part, however, giants are evil and monstrous creatures, feared for their great size and strength and, of course, for their fondness for eating people.

Godzilla

If ever a monster was born to battle, it is *GODZILLA* – a radioactive, fire-breathing, green lizard invented by a Japanese film company in 1956. Godzilla is a 500-feet-tall amalgam of sea-living lizard and dragon. So far he has been featured in eleven films, all of which revolve around his furious, city-destroying fights with other hairy, slimey and malevolent creatures. His most famous match was undoubtedly against King Kong although neither could be said to have won outright. Among his other famous opponents are Ghidrah, a three-headed monster from outer space, a giant female moth and the Smog Monster, a living collection of waste material that thrives on pollution. Against these lesser foes, Godzilla is always the victor.

Golem

The man of stone who suddenly comes to life is a familiar and popular theme in legend and literature. Its basis is in the Jewish myth of the *GOLEM* which is known in many versions. The Rabbi Elijah is said to have fashioned a man out of clay and to have given it life by writing the secret name of God on its forehead. The Golem then grew to giant size and became totally destructive. It could only be stopped by erasing the magic name. Another version of the story, set in Prague, maintains that the Golem was given life to protect

right: Godzilla, destroyer of cities, monster king.

46

the Jews who lived in a ghetto. When its work was done it became a statue again and was kept in a synagogue.

The Golem, or man of stone who can crush anything in his path and who lumbers along on stiff stone legs was a popular character in early monster films. Usually he was activated, or given life, by placing the magic word in an amulet around his neck. When this is removed he crashes lifeless to the ground. Like other favourite movie monsters, the Golem, or *It* as he was called in a more recent version, is virtually indestructible and will no doubt be revived many more times.

There is an obvious connection between the Golem and the Stone Guest, a similar legend which is best known today in Mozart's opera *Don Giovanni*. The statue of the man Don Giovanni has killed, returns at the end of the opera and clasps his killer's hand in an icy, terrible grip and drags him down to be consumed in the raging fires of Hell.

Gorgo

Just for a change, another cinematic, prehistoric, lizard-like creature wrecked London, rather than Tokyo or New York. This mammoth monster was *GORGO*, in search of her baby who had been captured and put on display by money-grubbing humans. Though a fairly predictable monster, bearing an obvious thematic resemblance to Mighty Joe Young and a physical one to Godzilla. Gorgo's spectacular appearance in Battersea Park and her fierce maternal instinct won her an affectionate following among monster fans.

Gorgons

In Greek mythology, the *GORGONS* were three terrible sisters called Stheno, Euryale and Medusa. Accounts of their appearance vary, although their common features are huge, vicious teeth, brazen claws and serpentine hair. Stheno and Euryale were as large as elephants and were immortal. Medusa had special attributes of her own.

In other versions, the Gorgons are represented as proud birds, or beautiful seductive women who lure men to their deaths. They were always terrible, however, because all three sisters could turn a man to stone with a single glance.

In the sixteenth century the Gorgon was believed to be a real monster, about the size of a small bull but covered with scales. It had enormous teeth, blood-shot eyes and a great mane of hair. It also had wings and hands and was supposed to live in Africa. Like the Basilisk it possessed a deathly breath and could kill with a look.

Grant

GRANT is the harmless-sounding name of a demon who was once popular in English myth. Grant resembles a large colt, but always walks on his hind legs. He has the traditional fiery eyes of a demon spirit. One unusual thing about this equine monster is that he lives and appears only in towns. According to legend, he would appear in the main street of a town at noon as a warning of approaching danger. Thus, although Grant was not himself notably malevolent, he was always associated with unpleasant happenings. Some people seem to have confused Grant with Grendel but there is actually no similarity between them at all.

Green Goblin

Goblins have always been regarded as tricksy, mischevious creatures, and these qualities are given a sinister twist in the character of the *GREEN GOBLIN*. For part of his existence he is a perfectly ordinary businessman but, like Dr Jekyll he cannot prevent himself changing into the wicked Green Goblin. He has the twisted, evil face and long pointed ears of the traditional goblin, but he rides around on a jet-propelled sky-scooter. He has a fund of magic tricks at his finger tips and spends most of his time trying to make Spiderman look a fool.

Gremlins

Leaving aside films and books which often give us new monsters, it is very rare for a mythological creature to enter the language of everyday life and for its origins to be clearly documented. All this,

right: The Golem chained up in a French film made in 1936 featuring Harry Baur.

The Green GOBLIN

UNLIKE MOST OF SPIDEY'S OTHER FOES, THE TRUE IDENTITY OF THE GRO-TESQUE *GREEN GOBLIN* IS STILL UNKNOWN! BUT, POSSESSED OF A FANTASTIC FLYING "BROOM-STICK" AND A WEALTH OF POWERFUL WEAPONS, IT IS CERTAIN THAT WE SHALL SEE MUCH MORE OF THIS DANGEROUSLY DIFFERENT EVIL-DOER IN THE NEAR FUTURE!

however, is true of the *GREMLINS*, whom we now instinctively blame when things go wrong. They are strange almost cartoon-like characters whose sole purpose is to annoy and upset people by making things, and especially machinery, go wrong.

They are said to be a combination of jack rabbit and bulldog – probably because they were 'discovered' by American and English airmen during the two great wars. They wear breeches and a red jacket, with spats and a top hat. They have very large feet and, according to some people, these are webbed like a duck's. Gremlins were first associated with the Air Force because they love to fly. Consequently they live in burrows near airfields so that they can sneak aboard airplanes unnoticed and create as much havoc as possible.

There is no end to the mischief caused by the Gremlins and no one is ever safe from them. Today their vexatious tricks are no longer confined to airplanes and their crew. We all know when the Gremlins are making things difficult for us.

Grendel

In Europe during the Dark Ages all evil giants, ogres and monsters were often said to be the children of Cain. One of the most grim and terrifying of these is *GRENDEL*, whose tragic

opposite: The Green Goblin from Marvel monsters.
below: This painting by Sir Edward Burne-Jones shows "Perseus and the Graie".

and frightening story is told in the ancient Anglo-Saxon poem, *Beowulf*.

The noble Dane, Hrothgar, built a magnificent hall in which he and his warriors feasted, sang songs and told stories. The noise of these nightly parties was said to enrage Grendel, a grotesque, semi-human giant who lived in a cave at the bottom of the Dark Lake. Grendel was attracted by the noise and lights and every night he attacked the great hall and killed thirty men. There was, in fact, a terrible feud between Hrothgar's court and Grendel which lasted many years. Each night the savage creature came to destroy and murder and no one could stop him for, by enchantment, Grendel could not be harmed by a sword.

At last, Beowulf himself came to the banqueting hall and swore to kill Grendel. When the creature arrived, he succeeded in killing one of Beowulf's men, but Beowulf woke up and seized hold of his arm. Despite the great strength of the creature, Beowulf hung on and would not let him go. With a superhuman effort, he tore Grendel's arm from his body and nailed it up as a trophy on the great roofbeam of the hall. Grendel slunk away to his lair and died of misery, for he had been deprived of his only pleasure – tormenting and killing the rejoicing inhabitants of Hrothgar's hall.

After witnessing his death, *Grendel's mother*, a monstrous hag, determined to avenge her son. She came at night to the hall and tore down her son's arm. Beowulf followed her and saw her disappear into the waters of the Dark Lake. Putting on his armour, he followed her. He was attacked by water serpents and dragged down by Grendel's mother. She carried Beowulf to her cave and there they fought a mighty battle. At last, Beowulf succeeded in throwing her to the ground, in spite of being wounded by her savage claws.

At that moment he saw an enormous sword on the wall and snatched it down. This was the only sword in the world that could penetrate the protective spell enjoyed by both Grendel and his mother. Beowulf killed the woman and then found Grendel's body. He hacked off the monster's head with the sword and carried it back to the surface of the lake. The head was so large that it required four men to carry it back to the hall in triumph.

left: London crumbles at the hands of Gorgo, the misused monster. right: The fabulous Gryphon of myth and legend.

Gryphon

The fabulous *GRYPHON* of India and Araby had the body of a lion with the head and wings of an eagle. Its entire body was feathered in black, red, white and dark blue. Each of its four paws had talons of enormous size and strength. The Gryphon was in fact supposed to combine all the attributes of the king of beasts and the king of birds. They fed their young on the bodies of dead men and themselves on horses, whom they hated above all animals.

Gryphons were widely associated with the guardianship of gold and precious jewels. According to legend they found gold in the mountains where they lived and built their nests of it. In these nests the Gryphons are supposed to have laid agates instead of eggs and to have stored other precious jewels which they defended ferociously against human marauders. Anyone who was brave and lucky enough to obtain a Gryphon's talon could recognize poison because the talon changed colour when it was placed close to a poisonous substance.

Hal

Stanley Kubrick's celebrated film *2001: A Space Odyssey*, contains the ultimate in technological monsters – a computer. This highly sophisticated piece of machinery is quite un-ghoulish in appearance, being a collection of dials, screens and keys. However, it has been programmed with a human voice, by means of which it communicates with the spacemen. Because of this human element the computer is at first affectionately known as *HAL*. Hal is in complete control of the ship. Its journey is so long that spacemen have been 'deep frozen' until required. Hal is responsible for maintaining their life-support systems, and for waking or thawing them when the time comes. Hal however, like so many man-made creatures becomes power-crazed and determines to do without the help of men. He therefore kills the frozen spacemen and plans to destroy those who are already awake. His eerie, unstoppable power is really chilling but his 'death', caused by disconnecting some of his circuits, is both sad and funny as the human voice falteringly sings 'Daisy, Daisy'.

Hameh

A curious variation on vampire-legends is found in Arabian mythology. It concerns a bird known as the *HAMEH* which is believed to spring from the blood of a murdered person. It has a monotonous and continuous call which means 'Give me drink'. The Hameh never rests until it has drunk its fill of the murderer's blood. Then it flies off to the land of dead spirits to deliver the news that the original death has been avenged.

left: Hal, the super computer from '2001: A Space Odyssey.' right: The winged Harpies lie in wait for unsuspecting travellers.

The Hameh might also be literally called, the voice of a guilty conscience.

Hands of Orlac

Originality in horror stories is hard to achieve. The *HANDS OF ORLAC*, however, provided a novel twist to the idea of surgical transplants. Orlac, a famous pianist, has to have his hands amputated. A familiar, typical mad doctor agrees to provide him with new hands. These have been taken, without Orlac's knowledge, from a murderer. The hands have a will of their own, and soon lead their innocent new owner into trouble. The story has been successfully filmed on two occasions and includes a horrifying apparition of the murderer. Having lost his own hands, he displays ugly steel ones and calmly announces that his head too, has been cut off, but that the mad doctor has succeeded in sewing it back on.

Harpies

A combination of vulture and woman, the four *HARPIES* were regarded as the embodiment of evil and were universally feared in Greek myth. Their wings and claws were made of brass and their human faces were perpetually pale with hunger. Everything they touched immediately became contaminated with a foul stench. They were sent by the gods to plague the blind King of Thrace, whose meals they snatched before he had a chance to eat. They were afraid of only one thing – the sound of a brass instrument which put them to flight.

Hound of the Baskervilles

The legend of the Baskervilles, tells how the wicked Sir Hugo Baskerville brought a terrible curse upon his family. Sir Hugo kidnapped a young woman, a yeoman's daughter, who lived on the desolate moors of Devonshire. She managed to escape, however, while he was carousing with his friends. When Sir Hugo discovered her flight, he declared that he would make a pact with the Devil if he could overtake her before she reached home. At once he set off across the moonlit moor. Soon he was followed by his friends who found him in a hollow. The girl had fainted with fear and standing over Sir Hugo, tearing at his throat, was a large and terrible hound.

This creature, the *HOUND OF THE BASKERVILLES* gives the title to one of Sherlock Holmes' most famous cases. All Sir Hugo's descendants have met mysterious deaths and the local people believe that the Hound from

opposite: The Incredible Hulk, from the world of Marvel super heroes. below: The curse of the house of Baskerville, is a huge dog said to haunt the family. Sherlock Holmes reveals it to be a plot.

above: Jason battles with the many headed Hydra.

hell, which can frequently be heard baying on the moors, is responsible. The latest potential victim, Sir Henry Baskerville, is saved at the last moment from the Hound, which proves to be completely mortal. It is, however, a terrifying and unusual creature. It is a cross between a bloodhound and a mastiff. It is black in colour and as large as a lioness. At the climax of the book it comes racing out of the fog, its eyes blazing and apparently breathing fire. Holmes and Dr Watson soon discover that its face has been daubed with phosphorous to make it glow in the dark. The enormous savage Hound is in fact, part of a complicated plot, which Sherlock Holmes soon unravels, to obtain the Baskerville estate and fortunes.

Hulk

A vast, muscle-bound green giant is *THE HULK*. His phenomenal, unstoppable strength, like his grisly appearance, is the result of exposure to those freak gamma rays again. He is really Bruce Banner, who, while rescuing his friend Rick Jones, came into contact with the rays. Now Rick Jones alone befriends this monster who does not really understand what had happened to him, nor why he is hated and attacked wherever he goes.

Human Torch

Another member of the Fantastic Four, Johnny Storm is more commonly known as the *HUMAN TORCH*. He is the brother of Sue Storm, otherwise known as Invisible Girl, and can turn himself into a human flame-thrower, flying through the air as a sheet of all-consuming flame.

Hydra

Quite apart from its formidable appearance, the *HYDRA* was immortal and therefore believed to be invincible. One of the most horrible monsters of Greek myth, it had a dog-like, scaly body topped with nine serpentine heads. Whenever one of these heads was cut off, two grew in its place – hence the confusion about how many heads the Hydra eventually had. The foul breath from these many heads killed many people. The task of killing the Hydra was one of Hercules' twelve labours. He succeeded by staunching or cauterising with fire the wound made when a head was cut off. This prevented the two new heads growing. One of the Hydra's heads was immortal, however, and when Hercules had chopped that off he buried it under a rock where it could do no more harm. The Hydra was one of the many monstrous children of Echidna and Typhon.

Ice Warriors

Mars is the original home of the *ICE WARRIORS*, but they have travelled about the galaxies and through time to take part in various adventures of the British TV series *Dr Who*. They are slow and cold and look rather reptilian. Their speech is hissing, almost asthmatic, probably because they need a special atmosphere, deadly to humans, in order to thrive. They like very cold temperatures and once tried to take over the world by changing its atmosphere.

Invisible Girl

Sue Storm, now married to Mr Fantastic also travelled in the ill-fated spaceship invented by Reed Richards and became a superheroine as a result. As a member of the Marvel comic's Fantastic Four she is known as *INVISIBLE GIRL* because she can make anything, including herself, become invisible. She is also able to will a force-field into existence and to hurl force-bubbles at her enemies. She is now a mother and, perhaps because of this, frequently steps down in favour of *Medusa* when the Fantastic Four are doing battle with their various enemies.

Invisible Man

Originally a powerful and convincing early science-fiction novel by H. G. Wells, the *INVISIBLE MAN* soon became a film favourite, not least because of obvious opportunities the theme presented for amazing trick photography. The Invisible Man was, inevitably, a scientist experimenting with a strange Indian drug. After injecting himself, he became invisible and quickly realized the new freedom this gave him. True to the monster tradition, he used his invisibility for evil ends.

In films, the invisible man is usually seen as a heavily bandaged man or as an apparently empty suit. The great moment of shock comes when the bandages are removed to reveal nothing. This is

below: Claude Rains starred in the Universal film of the Invisible Man made in 1933. The heavy bandages disguise the 'nothing' inside.

probably the classic example of the unseen menace being more frightening than the most repugnant creatures.

It came from beneath the sea

In the film *IT CAME FROM BENEATH THE SEA*, it was, in fact, a giant octopus contaminated by radio-active fallout, produced by H-bomb tests. The creature itself became radio-active and as a result, its normal prey fled from it. Starving and angry, the octopus took to a diet of human beings to satisfy its hunger and vented its fury by wrecking the Golden Gate Bridge and a good part of San Francisco. A marine biologist announced that it could only be killed by having its central nervous system severed at a point just above and between the eyes. After the creature was driven back into deep water with the aid of flame throwers, two submariners succeeded in stunning the monster with a bomb, before harpooning it in the fatal spot. Fixed to the harpoon was a time bomb which eventually rid the world of this tentacled menace.

It came from outer space

In the heyday of the science fiction film, many creatures were given vague names like It, Thing and Them. In one film, *IT CAME FROM OUTER SPACE* in a ship which crashed into the Arizona desert. Originally, the ship was mistaken for a meteor, but on investigation its true nature was discovered. The door of this vessel opened and then closed. Nothing, apparently, had left or entered it. Later, however, the young scientist investigating the mystery, sees a strange ecto-plasmic creature with a single, large eye. It begins to take people into mental captivity, turning them into virtual automatons. Only then does It reveal that it wishes to have time to mend the damaged spaceship and that, while it intends no harm to the people of earth, it is holding a number of hostages until the repairs are completed. The local people will not accept this and organize a posse to attack the ship. Then It materializes as a mass of shapeless jelly-like substance with a single eye. The scientist succeeds in blowing up the spaceship and It returns to space

as a ball of blinding light. All the hostages are instantly returned to normal.

top: An Ice Warrior from the television series Dr. Who. bottom: Tony Harwood as an Ice Warrior in the final episode 'The War Games'. opposite: Victoria faces Varga, the leader of the Ice Warriors.

Jekyll and Hyde

Like many of the great horror classics of literature, Robert Louis Stevenson's *The Strange Case of DR JEKYLL AND MR HYDE* is an entertainment with a high moral purpose. It is Stevenson's attempt to explore the fact that a man is made up of both good and bad instincts. This idea fascinates Dr Jekyll, a respectable, rich and intelligent man, who recognises in himself certain bad traits. By releasing these, with the aid of a mysterious chemical formula, he discovers that the bad instincts are greater and more powerful than the good. Evil destroys everything, including itself.

Written in 1885, the idea for the book is said to have come to Stevenson in a dream – or rather nightmare – and he wrote the book very quickly, locked away in his study. The popularity of the story has robbed the original of nearly all its mystery. It is impossible to read the book today without foreknowledge of the fact that Jekyll and Hyde are one and the same person. This crucial fact, however, is concealed until the closing pages of the book.

We first hear a strange story of a man of 'unexpressed deformity' who tramples a little girl to the ground one dark night in London. He is apprehended and made to pay compensation, which he does with a cheque signed by Dr Jekyll. Mr Utterson, Jekyll's friend and lawyer, knows that the Doctor has made a strange will leaving everything to Edward Hyde. Soon afterwards, Hyde is observed in an act of brutal and senseless murder. Immediately after this he disappears. Later, we learn that Jekyll has lost control of the ability to change into the evil Hyde. It can happen without his taking the medicine he had discovered. Now the formula is only needed to change him back

below: Comedy when Abbot and Costello meet Dr. Jekyll and Mr. Hyde. opposite top: Spencer Tracy about to be transformed. opposite below: Frederic March won an oscar for his performance.

into Dr Jekyll, and he needs ever larger doses. Eventually, he runs out of the formula and is unable to obtain the right ingredients to make more. He is doomed forever to be the murderous Edward Hyde who 'alone in the ranks of mankind, was pure evil'. At the last moment, fearing that he will be hung for his crime, Hyde commits suicide and the truth is discovered among Henry Jekyll's papers.

Unlike most monsters, Mr Hyde is not visibly malformed. The horror he strikes in people is the result of something they sense rather than see. 'Mr Hyde was pale and dwarfish, he gave an impression of deformity without any nameable malformation, he had a displeasing smile, he had borne himself to the lawyer with a sort of murderous mixture of timidity and boldness, and he spoke with a husky, whispering and somewhat broken voice: all these were points against him, but not all of these together could explain the hitherto unknown disgust, loathing and fear with which Mr Utterson regarded him. That can only be explained by the unadulterated evil of the man.

As we can see from this description, the hairy, werewolf like Mr Hyde is a creation of the cinema. He was first portrayed on both stage and film without the benefit of elaborate make-up. The actors concerned simply twisted their bodies into hunched and dwarfish shapes, altered their voices and, no doubt, pulled horrible faces. This was undoubtedly a considerable feat of the actor's art, but with the development of trick photography it soon became obvious that a much more terrifying Mr Hyde could be presented. Thus Stevenson's idea of moral evil gained a physical shape which has varied with each successive film version. In the same way, the story line has been altered to suit box-office demands, with the result that Dr Jekyll and Mr Hyde have both strayed far from the original book. As with *Frankenstein*, the horror elements in the original story have been developed quite separately to make a vehicle of chills and thrills.

In one respect, however, the film makers have remained fairly true to Stevenson. The smoking, foaming mixture which brings about the terrible transformation, and the writhing contortions of the change itself correspond closely to Stevenson's own highly dramatic description.

'He . . . measured out a few minims of the red tincture and added one of the powders. The mixture, which was at first of a reddish hue, began, in proportion as the crystals melted, to brighten in colour, to effervesce audibly, and to throw off small fumes of vapour. Suddenly and at the same moment, the ebullition ceased and the compound changed to a dark purple, which faded again more slowly to a watery green . . . He put the glass to his lips, and drank at one gulp. A cry followed; he reeled, staggered, clutched at the table, and held on, staring with injected eyes, gasping with open mouth; and, as I looked, there came, I thought, a change; he seemed to swell; his face became suddenly black, and the features seemed to melt and alter – and the next moment I had sprung to my feet and leaped back against the wall, my arm raised to shield me from that prodigy, my mind submerged in terror.

"Oh God!" I screamed, and "Oh God!" again and again; for there before my eyes – pale and shaken, and half fainting, and groping before him with his hands, like a man restored from death – there stood Henry Jekyll.'

Although Robert Louis Stevenson's story was entirely original, the idea of man's duality and his ability to change shape is by no means new. There are elements of werewolf legends in the tale, a fact which, to look at the make-up adopted by many actors who have played the part, has not escaped movie directors and make-up men. Not quite all the cinema Hydes have been wolf or ape-like, however. In a 1920 film version, John Barrymore 'modelled' Mr Hyde on a hideous spider. To underline this point, a sequence was added in which a huge spider crawls onto Jekyll's bed and melts into his body. When he wakes up he finds that he has involuntarily changed into the foul Mr Edward Hyde. And in 1941, Spencer Tracy gave perhaps the most subtle Hyde performance without any physical deformity whatsoever.

Jinns

Long before men appeared on the earth, the world was populated, according to Muslim myth, by evil spirits called *JINNS*. These demon spirits were supposed to have been born of fire, but they challenged the authority of God and were punished by banishment to the desert. They are expert shape-changers, but prefer to conceal themselves from men. Animals can see them when they stalk abroad at night. On the few occasions when they have been sighted by men, they have appeared as a combination of wolf and hyena.

above: The Kraken attacks a passing sailing ship.

Kelpie

Scottish legends frequently tell of the *KELPIE* or Water Horse, a creature supposed to be in league with the Devil, who is full of black evil. Descriptions of this creature vary, but it is usually represented as a black cross between horse and bull, with two sharp horns. The Kelpie is a shape-changer and frequently appears as a beautiful, tame horse, with a fine saddle and bridle, quietly grazing beside a loch or river. When anyone mounts this creature, it immediately gallops into the water and drowns its rider. Then it feasts on the drowned person's flesh.

In other, equally popular versions of these legends, the Kelpie transforms itself into a handsome young man. In this shape it woos young women, only to lead them to a watery grave. However, in human form the Kelpie's hair is always wet and often has waterweed and sand tangled in it. There is nothing the Kelpie can do to conceal this and so any young woman who notices it is warned of her lover's true identity and can escape.

There are many ancient stories about a gigantic black water horse which lives in Loch Ness. These tales may have contributed to belief in the Loch Ness Monster.

Keres

When the implacable fates had fixed the hour of death, the *KERES* would appear to do their will. According to Greek legends, the Keres were most often seen hovering over the field of battle. They wore red robes and had dark skins which accentuated their sparkling eyes and vicious white teeth. At the moment of death, the Keres would let out a chilling cry and descend upon their victim, drinking the streaming blood from his wounds. Afterwards they would carry the body down to the underworld.

King Kong

Few monsters have achieved the lasting popularity of *KING KONG* whose long and spectacular life began in 1933. In order to produce the film that was to launch him, no less than twenty-seven models were made, in varying sizes, to achieve the realism which made Kong seem more real than his human co-stars. Of course, this was only achieved by the most painstaking work. The models had to be photographed every time their position was altered by as little as one sixteenth of an inch.

Kong is, of course, a huge gorilla, fifty feet high, with an armspan of some seventy-five feet. He was discovered on Skull Island, which lies somewhere in the ocean, south-west of Sumatra. Skull Island is one of those accidents of nature, where prehistoric monsters have survived as a result of isolation. The native inhabitants of the island lived in fear of Kong whom they sought to placate periodically by giving him a human bride. Fay Wray, who played Kong's leading lady, was brought to the island by an interpid film-maker and explorer. Her fair hair and skin was particularly attractive to the gorilla who tenderly picked her up and hurried back to his remote mountain lair. Although pursued by men and attacked by other gigantic predators, Kong showed a strange gentleness and affection towards his blonde 'bride'. Kong was unstoppable until bombarded with gas bombs to which he finally succumbed. Then, setting a pattern followed by many other prehistoric monster movies, Kong was shipped back to New York and put on public display. Enraged by the popping flashbulbs of news-hungry photographers, and filled with an almost human longing for his definitely human sweetheart, Kong broke free and snatched up his prize and took her on a nightmare journey to the top of the Empire State Building. There, in the film's most famous scene, he is eventually gunned

right: King Kong with his 'bride' in New York.

down by airplanes, but not before he has successfully swatted at several, as though they were so many annoying summer flies.

'King Kong' contains a strong element of allegory. The familiar theme of man's lack of respect for the animal kingdom is joined with the ancient idea of Beauty and the Beast. Kong's gentleness and affection for Fay Wray is distinctly touching, while her power over him – the fatal attraction of beauty – is the cause of his ultimate downfall.

Kong, in the time-honoured tradition of money-spinning movies, has been given a son and was revived to do battle with Godzilla. However, none of his later incarnations has duplicated the awe-inspiring sight of his first lumbering appearance on the screen, or his final tragic death in the unwelcoming streets of New York.

Kraken

The Norwegian *KRAKAN* is a gigantic sea-monster, over one and a half miles long. It has hundreds of tentacle-like arms and is really a sort of mythological octopus or giant squid. It is said to spend most of its time sleeping on the bottom of the sea, but when it awakes it rises up, wrecking ships and devouring people. When it subsides again its vast bulk causes a deadly whirlpool to form. The legend has been extended in terrifying contemporary science fiction terms by John Wyndham in his famous book *The Kraken Wakes*.

Kronos

KRONOS is both the name of a mythological Greek giant and of a monstrous machine featured in the film of that name. The machine is a huge cube-shaped object with a revolving satellite for a head which is sent to earth, from a dying alien planet, to collect and transport the energy they so badly need. This complicated manoeuvre requires two mini-invasions of earth. The first occurs in the form of a ball of light which transplants an alien intelligence into a human body. The second, an asteroid, crashes into the sea, causing a tidal wave, and delivering Kronos to earth.

The creature is controlled by the alien intelligence and acts as a sort of monstrous robot vacuum cleaner, collecting all the energy it can

find. This causes it to grow bigger and bigger and to destroy everything that crosses its path. When the scientist who is playing physical host to the alien mind is killed, Kronos is uncontrolled and uncontrollable. It approaches Los Angeles on the track of a large atomic stockpile.

At the last moment it is discovered that electronic dust produces a chain reaction in the great machine which puts it out of action. It is therefore, attacked by jets which bombard it with this dust, thus saving the world from another terrible science fiction fate.

Kong is bombed on the Empire State Building.

Ladon

One of Hercules' fabled tasks was to steal the Golden Apples of the Hesperides which were jointly guarded by three lovely maidens and the monster *LADON*. Ladon was a hundred-headed dragon. He had the gift of human speech and never slept. His monstrous form and eternal wakefulness were, however, no match for Hercules who killed him and took the Golden Apples.

Lamia

A beautiful Queen of Libya was once loved by the god Zeus. He gave her the power to remove and replace her eyes at will. The goddess Hera killed all the queen's children and for ever after she ate any children she could find. This queen's name was *LAMIA* and she was half serpent and half women.

Later versions of her life cast her as a treacherously beautiful snake which seduced young men in order to kill them. This legend formed the basis of John Keats' famous poem *Lamia*. Despite the

Lamia, Queen of Libya, half-woman, half-serpent.

death of her first children, she is said to have had many terrible offspring called Lamiae. These were blood-sucking creatures, half human and half serpent, with four feet. The front feet had claws and the back were cloven hoofs. Other stories about Lamia's descendants describe them as a combination of goat and horse. These creatures lived in dark forests and only emerged at night in order to bite human beings. Those bitten in this way could only be cured if they heard the Lamia's roar.

Leshy

In Slavonic mythology, the *LESHY* was the reigning spirit of a forest. There were, therefore, many Leshies, one to each forest. All were shape-changers. Deep in the heart of the forest, the Leshy would stride along as tall as the tallest tree, but when he visited the edge of his domain he would make himself so small that he could hide

under a leaf. The Leshy was mainly human in appearance, but anyone could recognise him by his blue complexion – the result of blue blood, which had no aristocratic connections – and his long, straggling green beard. His eyes were also green and they seemed to be about to pop out of their sockets. Some people maintained that Leshies always wore their shoes on the wrong feet and buttoned their clothes the wrong way round.

Leshies were more mischevious than evil. If anyone wandered into the forest the Leshy would lead them astray, confuse them and generally make a nuisance of himself. However, Leshies did not actually harm people and you could always escape their annoying spells by sitting under a tree, taking off all your clothes and putting them on again back to front. It was most important to remember to put your shoes on the wrong feet.

Another curious fact about Leshies was that they always disappeared in October, Some said they 'died' temporarily. They would return in force in the spring, however, when they were particularly troublesome.

Lizard

Like the mysterious mutants who became *The Alligator People*, Dr Curtis Conners changed into a *LIZARD* when he drank alligator serum in an attempt to grow a new arm to replace one he lost in an accident. Now he is a man-sized lizard and one of Spiderman's fiercest enemies in Marvel comics. Spidey knows that inside the Lizard's horrible, scaly body is the demented mind of Dr Conners. He therefore tries not to harm this enemy and is constantly seeking a formula that will enable him to become an ordinary human again.

Loch Ness Monster

Stories concerning the presence of some gigantic monster or *Kelpie* living in the deeps of Loch Ness are as old as man, and at least one of them is better authenticated than most. Centuries ago, when St Cummein established a monastery on the banks of Loch Ness, one of the monks refused to plough the land because he said it was not suitable work for monks and that God should provide if He wanted the fields cultivated. According to legend, the fields were ploughed at night by an enormous black horse which then carried the rebellious monk off into the depths of the loch. Later it was said that the monster helped St Columba to cross the loch and, as a reward, was granted the freedom of the vast stretch of water by the saint.

The creature's unusual connection with saints is mentioned again in a written account of St Columba's life. Columba was an early Christian missionary who travelled to Scotland in AD565. A written record tells how he came upon a group of men burying one of their fellows beside the loch, who had been killed they said, by a monster. Their boat was now floating unmanned in the water. Columba ordered a man to swim out and fetch the boat, but the monster suddenly broke the surface of the loch and threatened the swimmer. Columba ordered the beast to go back and to leave the man alone. Then he made the sign of the cross and the creature swam rapidly away.

This account was written by an educated and reliable early historian and therefore differs from legends which are usually passed on by word of mouth and which become altered and exaggerated by repeated tellings. No doubt stories about some unknown loch-dwelling creature continued to be told and believed but the *LOCH NESS MONSTER* as we think of it today really dates from 1933. During that year, it has been estimated that between twenty and thirty different reports were made by people who saw something swimming in the loch. This large number of sightings resulted when a major road was under construction along the lochside. This involved the use of dynamite which may have disturbed or awakened the creature. Certainly the normally peaceful and remote loch was unusually noisy and well-populated at that time.

Since then many more sightings have been reported. Even more have probably never been mentioned because the absence of scientific proof of the monster's existence has caused most people to treat the subject as a joke. However, since about 1957 the monster has been taken more seriously. Films and pictures as well as eye-witness accounts have been published which certainly indicate the presence of something in the loch. There is now a formal Loch Ness Investigation Bureau which studies the monster and tries to prove or disprove its existence with up-to-date scientific methods.

right: The Loch Ness Monster? Taken in 1934.

It is certainly possible for a large and even an unknown creature to live in Loch Ness. Hundreds of years ago the loch was like a Norwegian *fjord*, an inlet of deep salt water penetrating far into the land. Sea creatures could, therefore, have entered it, perhaps to breed. As the mouth of the loch became silted up, some may have been trapped. Very slowly, of course, the nature of the water would have changed from salt to fresh, but it is known that creatures can adapt to this sort of environmental change. We also know that creatures previously thought to be extinct have survived in exceptional circumstances and usually in remote places. The loch is very large, reaching in places to a depth of nearly one thousand feet. It is also likely that there are large underwater caves around its banks. It could easily contain and even conceal a very large creature. Finally, there is an abundance of large fish in the loch which could easily provide the monster with an ample food supply.

The great size of Loch Ness and the fact that its waters are impenetrably dark due to peat staining make observing and tracking the monster extremely difficult. With one exception, therefore, sightings have occurred only when the monster has shown itself. It has been observed swimming, basking on the rocky edge of the water and even on land!

The majority of sightings seem to agree on two points, Firstly, that the creature leaves a distinctive V-shaped wake when it swims, and secondly that a hump or several humps stick up above the surface of the water. Obviously, descriptions of the monster vary and it is impossible to say exactly what it may look like. By taking the common features mentioned in many reports, however, it is possible to suggest something of its general appearance. It seems to have a long, serpentine neck with a rather small, flat and ugly head. There are usually reported to be at least two humps on its sinuous and very flexible back, and it has a long tail with which it sometimes thrashes the water. It would certainly seem to be dark in colour, probably dark grey, and those who have seen the beast at relatively close quarters have described its skin as rough and rather like that of a toad. The most astonishing thing about the creature is its size, for although estimates differ it seems that it must be at least forty feet long.

To this imaginary picture of the monster we can add flippers, not only on the grounds of logic – it must have some way of propelling itself through the water – but because of an extraordinary under-

water photograph taken in 1972. An underwater sonor device, linked to a camera and strobe lights, was used in an experiment which, it may be said, took the monster by surprise. There is now in existence a photograph of part of some very large creature, showing what appears to be a fin or flipper some six to eight feet long and probably two to four feet wide. At the time this photograph was taken by the automatic equipment, the sonor device clearly registered the presence of an unusually large object moving near the camera.

What sort of creature the monster of Loch Ness is we cannot say with any certainty. Perhaps it will turn out to be some familiar water creature, or it may be some long-forgotten beast that has, by freak circumstances, survived in the mysterious waters of the loch. Most exciting of all is the quite serious possibility that it may be a creature hitherto unknown to man. With modern scientific equipment and so much genuine interest in the monster the mystery must surely be solved. In the mean-

time, we can be certain that there is something lurking in the depths of Loch Ness, something that can cause an unusual wake and which occasionally shows itself to the astonished eyes of observers.

Lybbarde

It is now generally thought that the Medieval *LYBBARDE*, mentioned in the legends of King Arthur, was a fictitious creature mistaken for the ordinary leopard. Once the mistake has been made, however, stories grew up about the beast, which was believed to be the offspring of a lioness and a male panther. The creature was so famous for its courage that it later became the heraldic symbol of boldness.

below: Medusa's hair was a mass of hissing snakes intertwined with frogs, but her face was beautiful.

Magnetic monster

A freak of science became the unforeseen threat in a film called *MAGNETIC MONSTER*. A new, unstable element was created by bombarding a radio-active isotope with alpha rays. The resulting substance upset magnetic fields and absorbed metal and energy at such a rate that it doubled its size and power every eleven hours. The scientists trying to cope with this dangerous element realised that it would eventually destroy the world if it could not be stopped. Fortunately, they hit upon the solution of feeding the substance on its own energy so that it became stable once again and was rendered harmless.

Mantichora

A creature resembling a lion with a horrible human face was once believed to live in India and to feast off people. The most unusual things about the *MANTICHORA* were its tail and its teeth. It had three rows of teeth in both the upper and the lower jaw, with which it would chew up anybody who happened to cross its path. Its tail was that of a scorpion, complete with deadly sting, but it was much larger. In addition, the tail contained quills or spines which the monster could 'fire' at its victim like arrows. In Spanish folklore, the Mantichora is a species of werewolf which eats children.

Medusa

Unlike her Gorgon sisters, *MEDUSA* was mortal and beautiful. She offended the goddess Athena, however, and her loveliest feature, her hair, was transformed into a hissing mane of snakes. Some descriptions maintain that she kept her beautiful face, although her eyes were cold and serpent-like and her hands and feet grew savage talons. In

other descriptions, she becomes a hideous winged monster, like her sisters. Either way she had the power to turn anyone she looked at to stone – in some versions because of her deadly, venomous eyes and literally fatal beauty, and in others by the sheer horror of her appearance.

Medusa lived in a cave, in front of which were the petrified bodies of her victims, like stone sentinels warning other travellers of the danger within. Her reputation spread throughout Greece and her destruction was thought to be impossible. A young hero, Perseus, rashly promised to bring Medusa's head to his benefactor, King Polydectes, when he was mocked for being too poor to buy the king a birthday present. He prayed to the goddess Pallas Athene who equipped him with magic sandals, an invincible sword, a polished shield, a cap that made him invisible and a bag. With the

above: The Mysterians, invaders from outer space terrorize the land in the film of the same name.

aid of these instruments he was able to reach Medusa's cave and to cut off her head with a single blow, without looking at her. He used the shield to reflect her image and so avoided her fatal glance. When he returned to King Polydectes' palace, however, he held the head aloft in triumph and the entire court was turned to stone.

Like many monsters from Greek mythology, Medusa is familiar as a character in American action comics. She is one of the race known as the *Inhumans* and her special weapon is her hair which she can will to stretch over long distances and use like a whip to disarm her enemies, or like a tentacle to overpower them.

Mermaids

MERMAIDS are a curious mixture of fact and fiction. It is now generally believed that seals with their human-like faces, are the factual basis for stories about Mermaids, while it is obvious that most of their behaviour has been borrowed from the legends of the Sirens. Half fish and half beautiful woman, the Mermaids are not particularly malevolent. Like the Sirens, however, their beautiful singing has been said to lure ships onto the rocks.

Mermaids are more usually presented as desirable creatures who frequently fall in love with sailors. Many legends claim that the Mermaid can shed her tail on land and if this is destroyed she will never return to the sea. A mermaid called Miranda was featured in two popular films some years ago which concerned her hilarious adventures on land.

below: The mermaids, women with the tails of fish. above right: The Minotaur devoured young men and women in the Labyrinth of King Minos.

Merwomen and Mermen are often said to be extremely ugly, with staring eyes and squashed up features, but even these creatures are not harmful to man.

Mighty Joe Young

Though frequently regarded as but a pale shadow of the colossal King Kong, *MIGHTY JOE YOUNG* remains one of the most endearing movie monsters. Unlike the majority of monsters, Mighty Joe is indisputably a hero. Raised by a rich young woman in Africa, he grew into a twelve foot high gorilla. His owner, who has ambitions to be a nightclub star, allows Joe to be exploited in her act. He suffers much provocation and eventually runs amok, spectacularly wrecking the nightclub and ending up in jail. The young women arranges for his escape and he redeems himself by rescuing a group of children from a blazing orphanage.

After this act of heroism, he is allowed to return to Africa where he lives happily ever after. Made in 1949, *Mighty Joe Young* is virtually unique among monster movies in that it displayed a conscience about the way unscrupulous human beings cash in on animals for their own gain, while missing out on none of the thrills and spills expected in a gorilla film.

Minotaur

In one of the most famous of all legends, Minos, King of Crete, is said to have begged Poseidon, the god of the sea, to send him a sign of his kingship. Poseidon granted his wish and a gigantic bull appeared out of the sea which Minos was meant to sacrifice to the god. He failed to do this and the enraged Poseidon made Minos' wife fall in love with the bull. The result of this love was the monstrous *MINOTAUR*, a creature so awful that it had to be hidden away in a maze beneath the palace of Knossos.

The Minotaur possessed a human body with the head and tail of a bull. Its roar was said to have struck terror into the hearts of all who heard it. There was good reason for this fear because the monster only ate human flesh. Part of King Minos' revenge on Athens was to demand a yearly tribute of seven youths and seven girls who were taken to Crete and sent into the maze. Since they could never find their way out, the Minotaur eventually

right: Provoked, Mighty Joe Young runs amok.

located and devoured them.

The hero Theseus delivered Athens and Crete from the Minotaur's reign of terror. He went as one of the annual sacrifices and killed the Minotaur in the maze. The princess Ariadne helped him by giving him a ball of thread which he unwound as he advanced into the maze. This enabled him to find his way out again – to a passionate but short-lived love affair with Ariadne.

Monolith Monsters

Fragments of black rock from a meteorite are discovered in the desert and found to have the power to turn human beings to stone. The rock chips do this by absorbing all the silicon in their victim's bodies. Silicon is the substance which keeps our flesh and skin supple. No sooner has the deadly secret of the rock been discovered than the entire area is flooded by a cloudburst. The effect of this water is to make the meteorite expand. It comes bubbling up from its crater and grows as tall as a ten storey building. It crashes to the ground under its own weight and shatters, but immediately each fragment begins to grow until there are dozens of these *MONOLITH MONSTERS* constantly falling, smashing and re-growing. As always in science fiction films, an antidote is found in time. The monsters are rendered dormant by salt water. Once this is known it is a comparatively easy matter to blow up a dam and flood the monster-infested area with the saline waters of a conveniently handy lake.

Monster that Challenged the World

The *MONSTER THAT CHALLENGED THE WORLD* was a giant mollusc of vaguely lobster-like appearance. It had a very large trunk-like beak for a face and eyes on stalks like those of the common lobster. According to the film to which it gave its name, the Monster was supposed to have been dormant, in a six foot diameter egg, at the bottom of the sea for billions of years. The egg was hatched by an earthquake, whereupon the creature started to slake its thirst by draining

human beings of their blood. In addition to its horrible appearance, described by one film critic as a giant, gelatinous slug, the monster leaves radio-active slime wherever it goes. Its existence is discovered by the U.S. Navy during man-ouevres and it is they who eventually destroy it with the aid of depth charges and limpet mines.

Morbius

The eternally chilling vampire legend has been given a new medical twist in the person of another arch-fiend from the world of comics, *MORBIUS*. As a normal human being Morbius suffered from a blood disease. In an attempt to find a cure, he was turned into a blood-crazy vampire. Now, in bat costume, he goes about his thirsty business and seems to be developing an alarming fondness for the blood of Spiderman. The invention of Morbius is an excellent example of the way in which age-old legends are perpetuated by being constantly revised and brought up to date.

Mummy

The Ancient Egyptian practice of mummifying their dead so that a bandaged but recognisably human 'body' remains has provided the cinema with another perennial monster. *THE MUMMY*, however, retains a flicker of humanity rare among monsters. According to most plots, he has been embalmed and buried alive and longs for his lost love. The Mummy is revived in one of two ways: either with the magic words written on the Scroll of Thoth, or by the life-giving juice of tana leaves. The story has been elaborated over the years, but the eternal Mummy is usually seeking or guarding his beloved princess. Lately, he has been found buried in swamps and has turned out to be bullet proof. Famous actors who have successfully terrified audiences as the Mummy include Boris Karloff, Lon Chaney and Christopher Lee.

Mutant from Metaluna

A film entitled *This Island Earth* told of the kidnapping of two nuclear scientists from earth be a denizen of the planet Metaluna. Metaluna was running out of its essential nuclear energy supply and was also under attack from the

residents of another planet, the Zahgons. The film is primarily notable however, for one of the costliest and ugliest monsters ever created. It was known as the *MUTANT FROM METALUNA*. It was the product of Metaluna's advanced technology and was designed as a worker robot. It was eight feet tall and was part human and part insect. The Mutant's vast mis-shapen head was mostly exposed brain which pulsated sickeningly every time its heart beat. This head was five times larger than the normal human head and had five interlocking mouths, one above the other. All the facial muscles were exposed and coiled like taut snakes over the head and neck of the creature. Its eyes were large and staring, while its long arms reached down to its ankles and ended in a single savage claw. The Mutant escaped from the doomed planet of Metaluna but, on entering the earth's atmosphere, it dissolved into a pool of green fluid.

Mysterians

Back in 1959 the *MYSTERIANS* invaded earth. They were a dying race of super-intelligent aliens from the planet Mysteroid. The object of their invasion was to capture human women, with whom they planned to repopulate their world. To aid them in their task they brought a giant Samurai robot, with eyes that gave out a deadly ray. *The Mysterians* was a successful Japanese science-fiction movie – hence the Samurai robot.

Mysterio

An unusual element of realism was brought into Marvel comics with the introduction of *MYSTERIO*. Mysterio is a special effects man, working in films and television and specializing in monster costumes. His work enabled him to copy Spiderman's costume and to commit a series of crimes in his identity. Now he wears his own costume, consisting mainly of a domed helmet and cloak which makes him look rather like a robot. He employs all the tricks of his trade in his battle against Spiderman, but like many more horrifying monsters, he cannot win.

opposite top: Boris Karloff is 'The Mummy' 1933.
opposite below: The Mummy strikes!

Nagas

A fabulous race of snakes is an unusual and monstrous feature of Indian mythology. These snakes are called *NAGAS* and are regarded as both powerful and dangerous. They sometimes assume human form, sometimes appear as fabulous snakes but most commonly they appear in the shape and form of ordinary reptiles. They are noted for their trickery, which is usually fatal to mankind whom they cunningly take by surprise. The king of the Nagas is named Takshaka and his rich and beautiful kingdom is said to be the glory of the underworld.

Nemean Lion

The first task of Hercules was to slay the *NEMEAN LION*, which terrorized the land around Mount Tretus where it lived. It was much larger than an ordinary lion and could not be killed by any weapon. Hercules managed to strangle the creature and thereafter always wore its skin as a sign of his bravery.

Nuckelavee

Centuries ago many Scots went perpetually in fear of a foul and ugly sea dwelling monster called *NUCKELAVEE*. This creature was half-man and half-horse, but the most awful thing about his appearance was that he had no skin on his body at all. His breath was said to spread disease and to have a disgusting smell. Fortunately there was some protection to be had from Nuckelavee. He was deeply afraid of running water which could therefore protect his potential victims.

below: Hercules fulfils his first task and slays the huge Nemean Lion, using only his bare hands to strangle the beast.

Dr Octopus

Otto Octavius was once a world-famous scientist who invented, among other things, a set of tubular, mechanical arms with which he could safely handle radioactive isotopes during his many experiments. One day there was an explosion during one of the experiments which fused the mechanical arms to Octavius's body and damaged his brain. The result was Marvel comic's evil genius *DR OCTOPUS*, who wants to dominate the earth. Ever since then, Doc Ock, as he is called by *Spiderman*, has been battling his way through a whole series of comic adventures. His many arms make him a fearsome adversary, but they frequently get him into difficulties, too.

Oni

In Japanese myths, the evil spirits or demons are called *ONI*. They have monstrous form. There are many kinds but among the most notable are the Oni of Hell. These creatures are green or red in colour and have oxen or horses heads with humanoid bodies. Their task is to hunt down and capture sinners whom they then transport in a chariot of fire to the presiding god of Hell. Another group of Oni are perpetually hungry and thirsty. Their stomachs are grossly swollen and they can change their shape and appearance at will. Some Oni are invisible. They seize the souls of the dead and appear to the bereaved relatives in the living form of the dead person. Oni are always malevolent and are said to be responsible for the spread of diseases.

Orcs

The late J. R. R. Tolkien's celebrated book, *The Lord of the Rings* has provided a whole new series of monsters, many of which have found a perma-

Dr. Octopus, the evil genius from Marvel comics.

nent place in popular contemporary mythology. One of the most important of these is a dwarfish elf-race known as *ORCS* who act as the main fighting force of the Dark Lord, Sauron.

There are two different kinds of Orcs. The most numerous are small, dirty creatures with disproportionately long arms. For the most part they are bow-legged and squint-eyed, while their teeth are like fangs. They wear leather clothing and iron shod shoes which are said to bespoil and blacken everything over which they pass. They communicate in a strange, hissing language and are very argumentative and quarrelsome, sometimes even eating each other when holed up in the black caves of Mordor which is their home.

Although these Orcs serve the Lord Sauron and fight his battles in great hordes, they are essentially cowardly and, when not doing battle, are very badly treated. They are often fed to the monster Shelob and the air-steeds of the Ringwraiths and they are frequently beaten. These Orcs have an abiding hatred of the sunlight which they will avoid at all costs.

The second species of Orcs are not afraid of the sunlight and were fashioned by the Wizard Saruman. They are larger, better fed and braver than the other Orcs. They are employed in Saruman's battle against Sauron but, despite their man-size and appearance and their bravery they are doomed to be outnumbered by the dwarfish Orcs.

Orion

Not all giants are foul and ugly. According to Greek mythology, *ORION* was an extremely handsome giant. He is said to have had a miraculous birth, springing from the earth where the gods, Zeus, Hermes and Poseidon, had buried the skin of a heifer. Orion was so large that he could walk on the bottom of the sea without getting his head wet. He was, of course, immensely strong and was famous as a hunter. He was blinded by the King of Chios for stealing his daughter, but was told by an oracle that he would regain his sight if he journeyed towards the sun. He was eventually slain by the goddess Artemis and he descended into Hades where his task was to hunt the wild beasts with a gigantic club. According to popular tradition, Orion was translated into a constellation of stars which shines brightly on winter nights.

Orthos

Cerberus, as we know, was a three-headed dog, but he had a less famous brother who was also a dog monster – this time with only two heads. He was used by Geryon to guard his herd of precious red cattle, but was clubbed to death by the mighty Hercules. The name of this two-headed monster was *ORTHOS* or *ORTHRUS*.

below: The Phantom's protegee in a faint.

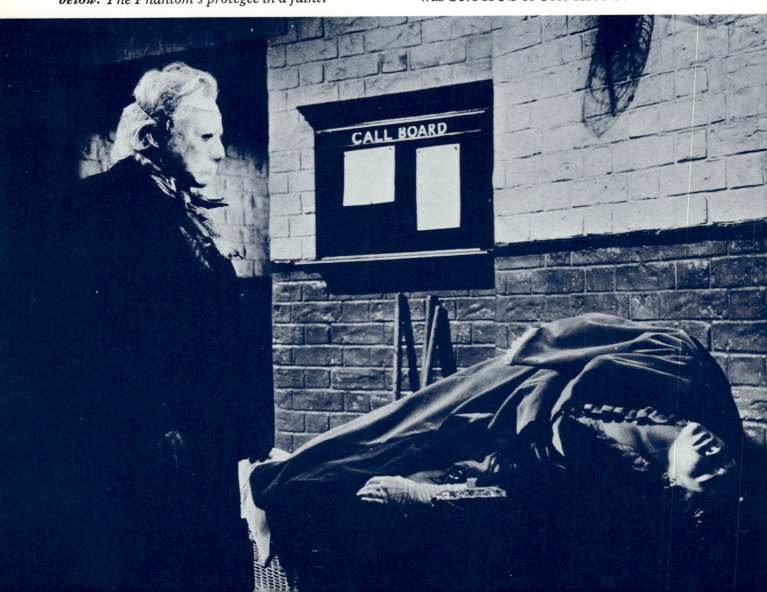

Phantom of the Opera

The *PHANTOM OF THE OPERA* is a man so ugly that he hides himself away in the catacombs of Paris and always appears masked and cloaked. He is a composer and lover of music. Consequently, he is drawn again and again to the Opera House, where he coaches a young girl who is singing in the chorus. When she fails to get her big chance, the Phantom is so angry he sends a vast, glittering chandelier crashing into the auditorium. Then he leads his young protegee to his underground lair, to listen to his music and to continue her tuition. She cannot resist unmasking him and is overcome with horror when she sees his evil malformed face. Some versions of the story say that the Phantom was made so ugly by being trapped in a fire. There have been several film versions of this tale, but it is generally agreed that the first version, which revealed Lon Chaney made up as a living skeleton, was the most horrific.

Polevik

In Russia it was once widely believed that every field was guarded and protected by a *POLEVIK*. Inevitably, descriptions of the Polevik varied from one part of the country to another. In some places he was simply a white-clad figure, but in others he was earth-black, with eyes of different colours and with long grass growing out of his ugly head. Most of the time, the Polevik was content to play tricks on people who trespassed into the fields, but if he ever came upon a drunkard, he would strangle him. The Polevik only approved of people who came to work in his fields, not to waste time or to recover from a heavy night's drinking. The Polevik usually had a wife and children and the youngsters used to catch birds who alighted in the fields to feed their parents. To escape the wrath of a Polevik, a

above: Lon Chaney as the Phantom, Universal 1925.
below: The Phantom lives as Claude Rains in 1943.
overleaf: Herbert Lom as the Phantom in 1962.

person had to place two eggs and an ageing cockrel that could no longer crow in the field as an offering. This had to be done secretly and then the Polevik would leave one alone.

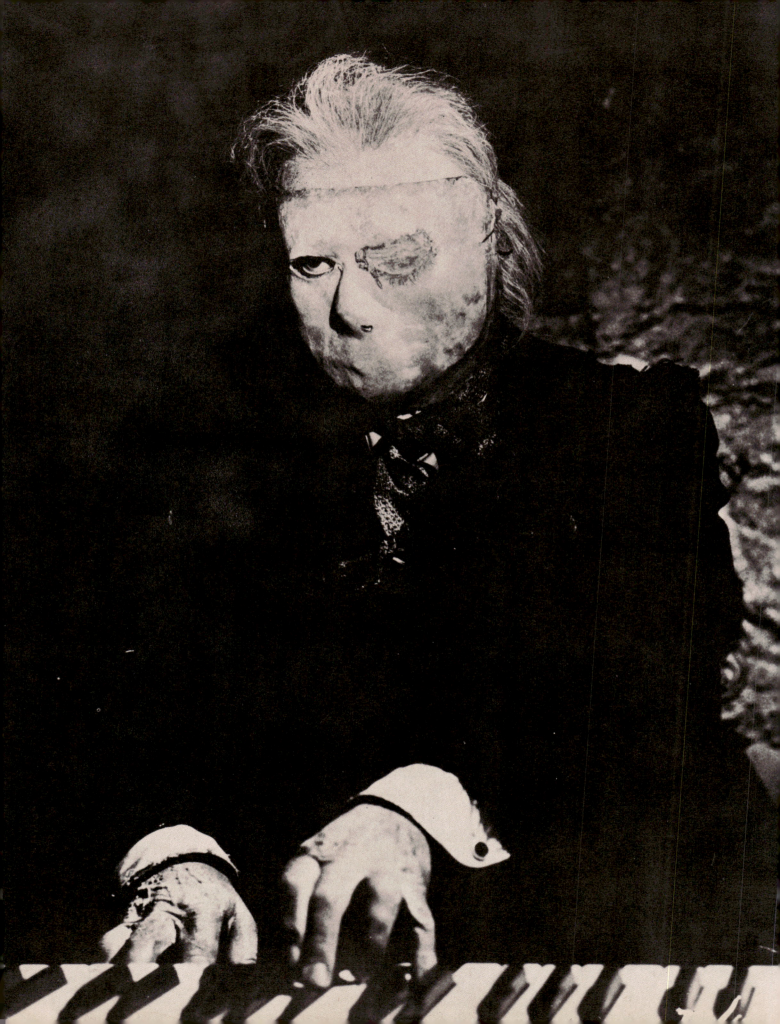

Quatermass

QUATERMASS is not the name of a monster but of a scientist who has had a great deal to do with monsters of varying kinds. Quatermass first appeared as part of the science-fiction boom in the 1950s, starting on television. The original plot concerned a returning spaceman who began to grow fungoid-like parts to his body and ended up as a giant, menacing vegetable. Adopted by the film industry, Quatermass has been involved with

The martians found inside the sealed compartment.

insect-like Martians and with bodiless aliens who take over human beings. The Quatermass stories were early examples of how science-fiction replaced familiar, lumbering creatures with ordinary but not less disturbing monstrosities.

Questing Beast

In the legendary romances concerning King Arthur, the *QUESTING BEAST* is described as having the body of a *lybbarde* with the hindquarters of a lion and a serpent's head. Its feet were borrowed from the deer, implying that it was a very fast creature. It was called a Questing Beast because its bay was said to be as loud as that of forty hounds. 'Quest' originally meant the baying of hounds in pursuit of their prey. Later, the chivalric quest was a task performed by a knight and this particular beast was the quest of Sir Palomides, one of the Knights of the Round Table. Today the beast is probably more familiar to us from T. H. White's *The Once and Future King* in which it is pursued by King Pellinore.

Redcap

There is a stooped, almost dwarfish old man, with long, ugly finger nails, who is said to haunt the scene of any violent encounter in the North of England. On his head he wears a red cap which obtains its colour from immersion in human blood. According to legend, it is very dangerous to visit a field of battle or a ruined castle at night for *REDCAP* longs to dip his cap into fresh human blood and does not mind killing in order to brighten up his headgear. Like most devils, he can be chased away by Holy Words or the sign of the cross.

Reptile

The ancient werewolf legend was reworked in a film entitled *THE REPTILE*. A young woman is the victim of a black magic curse, with the result that periodically she turns into a human snake, with a vampire-like tendency to sink her fangs into the throats of her victims. The transformation was accomplished without the aid of much make-up. The actress, Jacqueline Pearce, wore a slinky, snakey gown and a horrible lizard mask which did not entirely obscure her human features. The terrifying effect of the Reptile was heightened by this semi-human appearance.

Rhino

One of the least fabulous but nevertheless horrible monsters in comics is the *RHINO*. Dressed in a rhinoceros suit, complete with horns, this arch-enemy is extremely ugly and enormously strong. His strength derives from his rhino suit and is such that he can walk through brick walls like a one-man demolition squad. Rhino's power is based on nothing more than sheer brute strength, however, so he is no match for the superheroes.

Ringwraiths

Nine black cloaked and hooded sorcerers of great age play an important part in the struggle which is the main theme of *The Lord of the Rings*. They are called *RINGWRAITHS* and are the most powerful element in Sauron's attempt to obtain his ring. They inhabit a place called Minas Ithil, which was once a valley of beautiful gardens, dominated by a white tower. Now this tower is a place of torture, the gardens are black and evil with gaping holes in the ground which give off poisonous gases. Even the water in this vale is undrinkable.

The Ringwraiths ride both powerful horses and airsteeds, vast black carrion-eating birds with enormous wingspans. These birds have excellent eyesight and are very fast. They are also able to fire deadly poisonous darts from their bodies as they fly. The Ringwraiths converse by means of a series of hisses and blood-curdling, high-pitched wails.

The leader of the Ringwraiths strikes terror into the hearts of all who come near him, even by his very presence. When he removes his hood however, only the most intrepid souls can withstand his immense, evil power.

Roc

ROC is the name of a gigantic bird. Some say that it is an immense eagle, others that it is a cross between an eagle and a lion. On one point everyone is agreed and that is its size. It is so large that it can carry young elephants in its talons. According to the Islamic classic, *The 1001 Arabian Nights*, Sinbad the Sailor had two encounters with Rocs.

The first was actually rather fortunate for the intrepid voyager. He had fallen asleep on a remote island and so missed his ship. Sinbad climbed a tree to look for any signs of life on the island. In the far distance he saw what he took to be a vast white dome. When he drew close to this object he found it perfectly smooth, at least fifty paces round and entirely without an entrance. Sinbad could not think what the object was, but

opposite above: The Reptile's victim is found dead.
opposite below: The sleeping Reptile is revealed.

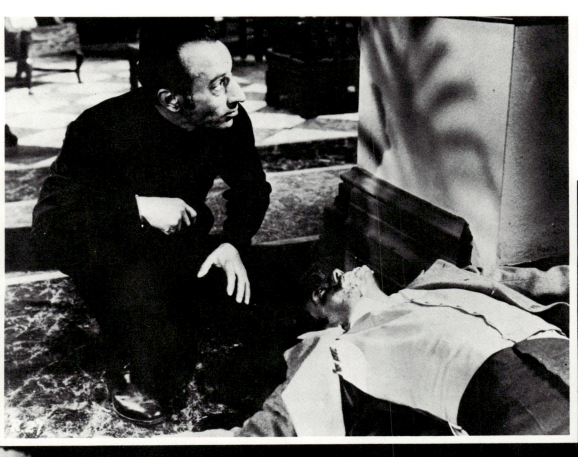
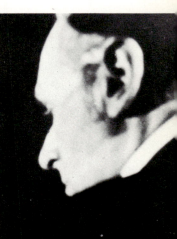

above: Sinbad ties himself to the leg of the Roc.

suddenly the whole sky grew dark with the approach of a monstrous bird. This was a Roc and Sinbad realised that the 'dome' was its egg. The Roc settled down on the egg and, quite unnoticed, Sinbad climbed onto its foot. The creature's leg was as thick as a tree trunk and Sinbad bound himself to it with his turban. The next morning the bird flew away, carrying Sinbad so high that he could not see the earth below. Suddenly it descended and Sinbad unfastened his turban and hurried away. The Roc had alighted to capture a serpent which it carried away in its beak. By hitching this unconventional ride, Sinbad escaped from the unpopulated island.

Sinbad's second encounter with Rocs occurred on his fifth voyage and was less pleasant. He and a group of merchants landed, after a long voyage, on another desert island where they immediately noticed another giant egg. They could see that it was about to hatch for the young Roc inside had begun to peck at it. Despite Sinbad's warnings, the merchants hacked the egg open with hatchets and roasted the young Roc. Later, two Rocs returned and seeing that their egg and baby had been destroyed, they became furious and flew off again in a great hurry. The captain of the two ships carrying Sinbad and the merchants put to sea at once for he feared the vengeance of the Rocs. They had not travelled very far, however, when the Rocs returned. Each carried a giant boulder in its beak. They dropped these onto the ships passing below. The steersman of one ship

managed to get his vessel out of the way, but the second was not so lucky. The boulder hit the middle of the ship, splintering it and casting crew and passengers into the sea. Sinbad was among these but, by clinging to a plank of wood, he survived to undergo more adventures.

Rosemary's Baby

Black magic and the occult have often been the cause of monstrous apparitions and happenings, and this idea was brilliantly exploited in the very ordinary setting of a New York apartment house in *ROSEMARY'S BABY*. Originally a highly successful novel, Roman Polanski's film version starred Mia Farrow as Rosemary – an ordinary young housewife who becomes unwittingly involved with a witches' coven who want the baby she is expecting. The Satanic powers of these outwardly ordinary people prove stronger than any help Rosemary can obtain and she actually gives birth to the Devil. The horror generated by *Rosemary's Baby* stems from the very ordinariness of the setting and characters which somehow make the diabolical rituals and plots of the coven uncomfortably believable.

Rusalka

Although she has a number of different forms, *RUSALKA* is always the spirit of a drowned girl. Legends concerning the Rusalki, who lived in the Danube, describe them as beautiful, moon-pale girls who, like sirens and mermaids, sang beautiful songs and lured people apparently to a not unpleasant death. In the northern parts of Russia, however, the Rusalka has the pale, waxy appearance of a drowned corpse and is only interested in seizing innocent people and drowning them horribly. For one week of the year, known as Rusalki Week, these spirits are supposed to leave the water and live on land. They like to hide in trees and can be heard playing and calling to each other. A Rusalka is supposed to make the ground more fertile when she treads upon it, but she can also be mischevious. She likes to destroy dams, stop mill-wheels and steal from sleeping human beings. The legend of these mysterious creatures has been immortalised in Dvorjak's opera *Rusalka*, which tells of the tragic love between Rusalka and a human prince.

Salamander

Many centuries ago, blacksmiths had a great respect for the *SALAMANDER*, a lizard that was said to live in fire. Blacksmiths therefore thought that salamanders lived in their forges and, as long as they were happy, the fire would burn well, but if anything upset the lizard, then the fire would go out and interrupt their work. Long before this, the Salamander was credited with the ability to extinguish fire simply by walking through it. Some people believed that their bite was poisonous and that the fire-proof substance asbestos was made from their skins. There is, of course, an actual lizard with this name but it does not possess any of these marvellous properties.

Sandman

In popular legend *THE SANDMAN* is a benevolent old man who puts children to sleep by sprinkling sleeping sand on their eyes. But in the action-packed world of adventure comics, Sandman is an arch-enemy of the superheroes and a member of the Fearsome Foursome. He has the ability to turn himself into a heap of soft sand or sometimes hard concrete at will.

Satyrs

Bacchus, the Greek god of wine, was said to be attended by half animal, half human creatures known as *SATYRS*. Originally, the Satyrs were represented as humans with distinctly animal faces and horns. They usually had the tail of a horse or goat as well. Later, they became confused with fauns and Centaurs and were shown with the lower body of a goat or horse. The Satyrs were minor gods in their own right. They represented the luxuriant and unruly forces of nature. From Bacchus they inherited their love of alcohol. When drunk, they could be extremely rowdy and liked to cause trouble.

Science Fiction Monsters

Three factors can be said to have caused the boom in *SCIENCE-FICTION MONSTERS* which dominated the cinema screen and, to a lesser extent, popular literature in the 1950s. The explosion of the first Atom bomb and the development of the Hydrogen bomb brought home to people the extraordinarily rapid and possibly uncontrollable progress of science and technology. The idea of space flight became a distinct possibility. Scientists predicted that a manned spaceflight would occur much sooner than most people expected and this fired the imaginations of artists and audiences alike. Finally, the threat of television made the cinema frantic for new and fabulous ideas. The horror movie had always been popular, but it needed revitalising.

left: The Salamander from an engraving.

above: Scylla snatching sailors from a passing ship.

Science-fiction films have used every possible kind of monster, but those which truly deserve the name are basically aliens from outer space. The plot usually concerns an invasion of planet earth, which brings evil and super-intelligent monsters to prey on practically defenceless human beings. Usually, these creatures have to be destroyed by the most sophisticated weaponry in all-out attacks. Sometimes the tension derives from a race against time to develop or discover some monster-destroying substance. In *The War of the Worlds*, however, the scaley boney-handed Martians were conveniently killed off by the common cold. It did not seem to worry anyone that the *INVADERS FROM MARS* had not the slightest resemblance to their predecessors. They were represented by giant domed heads, with vile, waving tentacles growing out of their shoulders.

Many invaders were virtually human. There was a tendency to give them large, domed, hairless scalps as a mark of superior intelligence, as in *THE PHANTOM FROM SPACE*, but other aliens, like the giant ants in *THEM* and the vegetable-like *GREEN SLIME* relied on more obviously horrific images.

Soon the decidedly unfriendly and unwelcome visitors had become disembodied objects, e.g. *THE FIEND WITHOUT A FACE* duplicated humans with alien powers, e.g. *Invasion of the Body Snatchers*, all kinds of Robots, including the specifically named *ROBOT MONSTER* and, eventually, invisible, mind-destroying forces. The visitors from outer space even infected or produced monstrous human children, as in *Village of the Damned*, who lived as aliens in our midst.

Science-Fiction Monsters have obvious advantages to film makers. Their origins can be left obscure, their powers and appearance can be as inexplicable and outlandish as the imagination can invent, and their demise can be engineered by the most unlikely or convenient means. The monstrosities of science-fiction are not bound by any human laws and so can be as outlandish or as ordinary as the individual director or writer wishes.

It is interesting to note that now that man has walked on the moon, the fantastic elements of science-fiction are much less popular. Science-fiction today is much more sophisticated and is more often concerned to duplicate the reality of man's greatest adventure, or to predict only that which seems probable in the very near future. The little green men and horrible, lumbering vegetables of imagination appear to have been eclipsed by our actual knowledge of space and other planets.

Scylla

SCYLLA was the victim of a jealous love which turned her into an avenging monster in Greek mythology. As a beautiful young girl she was loved by Glaucus, one of Jason's Argonauts. She spurned him however, and he enlisted the aid of Circe, an enchantress, who was so jealous that Scylla should attract Glaucus that she filled the sea in which the young girl regularly bathed with horrible serpents. By enchantment, these serpents became a part of her body, transforming her into an ugly six-headed monster. After this transformation, she lived in a cave on the coast of Sicily and fed on sailors whom she snatched from passing ships by extending her long, snakey necks.

Legend always couples Scylla with Charybdis, a rushing whirlpool in the straits between Sicily and Italy which further menaced the seafarers in that part of the world. The story is commemorated by the saying 'to be between Scylla and Charybdis' – which means to face two equally unpleasant alternatives.

right: Gorgo rising from the ocean is fantasy, but true sightings of sea serpents have been recorded.

Sea-serpents

'There must be still remaining in the depths of the ocean undescribed species of fish, of bizarre form, and probably gigantic size . . .' wrote Charles Gould in 1886. It is a belief shared by many who maintain that it is only a matter of time before the ancient mystery of the *SEA-SERPENT* is solved.

The oceans are vast and largely unexplored. Although we can cross them with ease, chart their currents and study many of the life-forms they support, whole areas of the sea floor remain undisturbed. The size of the oceans, the inaccessibility of much of their depth, and the fact that they contain an abundance of food means that it is perfectly possible for unknown and large creatures to live and breed there unobserved. There is, in short, no physical reason why sea-serpents should not exist.

Historical references to and belief in sea-serpents are as old as man himself. The Greek philosopher Aristotle mentioned vast creatures which attacked and overturned galleys off the coast of Libya and he has been followed by literally hundreds of others. Sea-serpents have been sighted all over the world and no coastal nation is without its particular legend of some ocean-dwelling monster.

Pontoppidan, Bishop of Bergen, was one of the first to collect evidence about sea-serpents. In 1755 he wrote at length about the Norwegian type, as it has come to be known, because of its apparent fondness for the deep calm *fjords* of Norway. Pontoppidan maintained that these

creatures lived on the bottom of the sea and only came to the surface in July and August when the weather is particularly calm and they are spawning.

About this time, sea-serpents were reckoned to be about two hundred feet long, twenty feet around the body and with a mane some two feet in length decorating the neck. Its body was scaled, its eyes fiery and it could raise its neck as high as a ship's mast. Occasionally, these monsters snapped people up from the decks and devoured them. Pontoppidan was reliably informed that these vast creatures had been known to rear up and throw themselves across ships in order to sink them. He doubted the truth of this however, and maintained that for all their size and strangeness they were very timid creatures who did their best to avoid ships and men.

Sightings of sea-serpents have been made regularly and many have been well authenticated.

To list all of them would require a book in itself. Some of the most reliable and remarkable, however, deserve to be mentioned in brief.

One of the most famous and most credible of sightings was that made by the captain and crew of *HMS Daedalus* in 1845. The ship was on a voyage from the East Indies when the serpent was seen. It was said to quite definitely resemble a snake. The head, which was carried about four feet clear of the water, was brown in colour with a yellowish-white throat. Its progress was rapid, but none of the observers could ascertain how it propelled itself along. In common with many other sightings, the creature appeared to have a sea-weed like mane and was thought to be about sixty feet long.

In 1872 two ministers of the church reported a series of sightings off the west coast of Scotland. At first all they saw was a black mass in the sea behind them. Then a series of humps appeared above the surface, with a regular interval between each hump. The creature accompanied them for some time. Sometimes three and sometimes six humps appeared. By careful observation, the gentlemen concerned estimated the creature to be about forty-five feet long.

One of the strangest of all reported incidents took place off the coast of Brazil in 1875. Again the sighting was made from a ship, the *Pauline*, and it concerned a battle royal between a sea-serpent and a large sperm whale. The monster was coiled twice around the body of the whale which it continually dragged below the surface of the water. During the struggle, the observers were able to see the tail and head of the creature which resembled a conger eel in colour. The battle lasted for some fifteen minutes before the whale was lifted vertically above the water, its tail lashing furiously, before being finally dragged down to the deeps.

The very antiquity of these reports may cause some people to dismiss them. More recent ones, however, do not in themselves contradict the detailed reports of past centuries. In 1963 two fishermen reported seeing a creature of great size and unknown type off the coast of Iceland. First two humps broke the surface of the water. The back or second hump was noticeably larger than the other. The length of body visible above the water was reckoned to be approximately fifteen feet and the largest of the two humps was about three feet from its highest point to the water line. The creature was black and shiny. It appeared clearly five times during the space of about fifteen minutes.

A year later another serpent was sighted off the Hebrides, this time from the land. At first the observer thought that the object he could see was a large box floating on the surface. When he got closer and used powerful glasses, however, he could see that it was the cow-like head of an aquatic beast, with its large body immersed below the surface. The head had a white lump on either side and the body was an estimated twenty-five feet in length, but did not resemble that of a snake. Instead the body seemed to be very thick, tapering a little towards the tail. The colour was grey and the skin was smooth. As is so often the case with such sightings, the witness could not tell how the creature propelled itself through the water.

Finally, Chay Blyth's companion, John Ridgway, with whom he rowed the Atlantic, reports seeing a thirty-five foot creature moving very swiftly through the water, which made a loud splash before disappearing. He was unable to give

left: '*The Great Sea Serpent*' *an impression of the monster by Hans Egede.*

93

many details because the incident happened at night and he only glimpsed the sea-serpent. His evidence is impressive however, because, like many other observers, he is a man with a vast knowledge of the sea and its known creatures. Thus there is little likelihood of his mistaking a known beast for a serpent.

All this evidence and much, much more has been collected together and scientifically examined by the French scientist and zoologist Bernard Heuvelmans. He has written an exhaustive and fascinating book, *In the Wake of the Sea-Serpents* in which he concludes that, when all the evidence has been sifted and analysed, it is possible to make a scientific pen-portrait of no less than nine different types of sea-serpent, all of which could exist without breaking the laws of known marine life. His analysis was made from three hundred and fifty eight sightings, all of which were found to be acceptable.

Forty-eight of these concerned the Long-Necked variety. Heuvelmans deduces that this is a cylindrically-necked creature, with a large body and four webbed feet. The back is apparently covered with rolls of fat which can give the appearance of humps breaking the water's surface.

THE MERHORSE has been reliably seen thirty-seven times. It too, has a long neck, but this carries a mane. It has large eyes and a bewhiskered face. The body shows only as a single hump.

THE MANY-HUMPED SEA-SERPENT is undoubtedly the one which appears as a row of barrels or a vertically undulating snake. Heuvelmans suggests that this species has a long row of humps all along its back. It has a flat, blunt head with a horizontal tail, similar to that of the whale, with the aid of which it can undulate vertically. These creatures vary between sixty and one hundred feet in length.

THE MANY-FINNED has been reliably reported twenty times. The creature appears to have a row of fins on either side of its body. These are probably excrescences of its body and according to Bernard Heuvelmans, would give it stability, since it lacks a prominent tail. This monster is thought to be between sixty and seventy feet in length.

Most of Heuvelmans' other classifications are self explanatory. *THE MARINE SAURIAN* is a crocodile of sea-going habits. The other types are the *SUPER-OTTER* the *SUPER-EEL* the *FATHER-OF-ALL-THE-TURTLES* and the

YELLOW-BELLY. This last creature is shaped like a giant tadpole and is yellow coloured with a broad black stripe down its back.

At the moment we cannot say definitely that these creatures live in the sea. However, they have been sighted and reported in detail by reliable and responsible people a sufficient number of times for Bernard Heuvelmans to arrive at these descriptions. Such creatures could live and hide in our vast oceans. On balance, therefore, we must admit that there is greater evidence for their existence than there is for them to be regarded as fantasies or mere legends.

Sirens

Many stories are told about the *SIRENS* who lured sailors to their death with their fatally attractive songs in classical myths. Some versions say that they were magically born from the drops of blood shed by Achelous, while in others they were beautiful maidens who prayed for wings in order to search for Persephone after she had been taken to Hades. Certainly they are represented as having human faces and breasts with the wings and legs of birds. They lost the power of flight when they dared to challenge the Muses to a singing contest, for the Muses plucked out their feathers in revenge. After this, the Sirens took to luring ships onto the rocks.

Despite their beautiful voices, they were often said to be hideous and pitiless creatures. If a man was able to resist the Sirens' song, they were doomed to leap into the sea where they were instantly turned into rocks.

A species of winged serpent supposed to have lived in Arabia was also called a Siren. It could fly as fast as a galloping horse and had a deadly bite.

Spiderman

One day a very intelligent but rather under-nourished-looking American teenager named Peter Parker was attending a lecture on radioactivity at his high school. Suddenly, a spider that had been affected by radioactivity descended from the ceiling and, in its death-throes, bit Peter Parker on the hand, creating a painful, burning sensation.

right: *Spiderman, super-hero, champion of good.*

Best wishes from your pal, Spidey

Thus, as millions of comic readers know, the fabulous *SPIDERMAN* was born. From that moment on the undersized youth inherited the super-strength and agility of a radioactive spider. Spiderman, or Spidey as he is affectionately known to his friends, can walk up sheer walls and across ceilings just like a real spider. And he can swing effortlessly from skyscraper to skyscraper in pursuit of his many enemies.

As Spiderman, Peter Parker wears a distinctive costume, fretted with webs and emblazoned with spider insignia. The most important part of his equipment, however, is his web-shooter. This is worn on his wrist and has a super-sensitive button projecting into the palm of his hand. One push of this button releases web-fluid, either as a single strong rope, a web-like spray, or as a gooey liquid. In any of these three forms, the web-fluid invariably incapacitates Spiderman's enemies, or helps him to escape from difficult situations. The agile, invincible Spiderman is an unflagging enemy of evil and one of the most popular of Marvel's comic strip superheroes.

Sphinx

The *SPHINX* combines the body and tail of a lion with the head and breasts of a woman. In addition, she has eagle's wings and was one of that large family of hybrid monsters bred by Typhon and Echidna. She was sent by the gods to punish King Laius of Thebes which she did by terrorizing and eating travellers on the roads around Thebes. The Sphinx demanded that every traveller should answer a riddle and if they failed to do so correctly, she promptly ate them.

When Oedipus encountered the Sphinx she asked him what creature had one voice, and walked first on four feet, then on two and finally on three. Oedipus answered that the creature was a man for as a baby he crawls on all fours, for most of his life he walks upright on two feet, but in old age he often leans upon a stick. On receiving the correct answer, the Sphinx hurled herself over a cliff and

left: This painting 'Oedipe et la Sphinx' is by Moreau. opposite top: From Star Trek, The Talosians. opposite left: The ancient robot-probe Nomad aboard the Enterprise. opposite right: The terrifying lady in this picture is the witch from the Star Trek episode 'Catspaw'.

died. Oedipus was welcomed as a hero in Thebes.

The more familiar Sphinx comes from Egypt and is associated with the sun god or the god of wisdom. In Egyptian lore, Sphinxes are male, but the Babylonians regarded the female Sphinx as a symbol of the moon goddess. In all versions, the Sphinx is connected with riddles and great wisdom. Her unpleasant habit of eating people is only found in the Greek legend.

Star Trek

On its mission to *boldly go where no man has gone before*, the star-ship *Enterprise* encounters many strange and alien creatures.

On a distant planet in the galaxy, Captain Kirk and his crew come into conflict with a horrible *SALT SUCKING MONSTER*. She lures her victims by assuming the form of a loved one, then motivated by her need for salt to survive, she sucks the salt from their bodies. She is destroyed at last, by Mr. Spock. As the image of a beautiful woman fades she becomes a terrible creature with a yellow skin and a decomposed body.

NOMAD is beamed aboard the *Enterprise*, where it is discovered that he is an ancient robot-probe who has been programmed to seek out and destroy all imperfect life-forms. This danger to the captain and crew is destroyed eventually when its mind is confused, causing it to self-destruct.

The *TALOSIANS*, an alien life form of diminutive size have large bulging heads which accommodate very advanced brains. They communicate by telepathy and as they do so their skulls pulsate sickeningly. Their most dangerous attribute is their ability to make their victim's most terrible nightmares reality, thus torturing them.

Stegosaurus

A remarkable illustration of the way nature helps animals to adapt to their environment is provided

by the *STEGOSAURUS*, one of the later dinosaurs. The creature was literally armour-plated, with a double 'frill' of bone-plates running the length of its spine. In addition it had a powerful spiked tail which it could use to beat off an enemy. These peculiarities were for its protection. The fact that it walked on all fours, with its rear end much higher in the air than its front is an example of adaptation of a different kind. The proximity of the Stegosaurus's head to the ground made it much easier for it to find the plants on which it lived. Dinosaurs, however, were not very successful at adapting their brains. The Stegosaurus had a very small head and an even smaller, extremely limited brain. To off-set this disadvantage it possessed what amounted to a second brain, seated in its lower spine. The conventional brain took care of the creature's nutritional needs, while the second operated its big hind legs and defensive tail.

below: The huge but quite harmless Stegosaurus.

Terrible Wild Monster

There is an extraordinary account of a monster which was supposed to have been killed just outside Jerusalem in 1725. The creature is unprecedented and unknown. In the contemporary account of its death, it is simply called, the *TERRIBLE WILD MONSTER*. For some time rumours had circulated of inexplicable devastation on Forest Mountain some fourteen miles from Jerusalem. Men, cattle and horses had all been savagely killed. In the space of a single month the monster is said to have killed forty-nine people. Eventually the creature was sighted by a traveller in the region who organised the local people to hunt it down. They, however, were so afraid of the creature that they sent for the army. The supposed eye-witness account of this beast describes it as follows.

The Terrible Wild Monster was as large as a horse and its entire body was covered with scales set so closely together that it was virtually armour-plated. These scales resembled mother-of-pearl. Its tail, which measured over four feet long, was like that of a Basilisk with a sting at the tip. Its head generally resembled that of a lion, but in addition, it had an eagle beak, teeth and long elephant-like ears. Its powerful feet were clawed and it had a spiney ridge, rather like the spurs of a fighting cock, running all down its back and hind legs. To top it all it had the wings of a serpent.

At the sight of this highly hybrid creature, the horses carrying the soldiers bolted or threw their riders. One soldier, lying on the ground in despair of his life, had the presence of mind to stick his lance down its throat and so the beast was killed.

The explanation offered by the contemporary manuscript for the origins of this monster may be considered as fanciful as its description. A prince of Tartary is supposed to have massacred a large group of people who had defied him. This was

done on Forest Mountain and their blood, fermented by the earth, is said to have given unnatural birth to this horrendous animal. The writer maintains that the beast contained the spirits of these slaughtered people and that its unprecedented cruelty is indicated by the fact that it killed, not to eat but only to drink the warm blood of its victims.

The Thing

In the late Forties, horror movies began to go out of fashion. Frankenstein, Dracula and the rest of the spooky crew were to return, but in the meantime science or rather science-fiction was the order of the day. One of the first films to capitalise on the rapidly developing technological age was *THE THING*. This alien monster had journeyed through space and been frozen at the North Pole. It was, of course, accidentally revived and began to terrorize the community. It was over eight feet tall and was quite inhuman. Its hairless body was found to have no nerve ends and therefore it could not feel pain as we know it. As a final touch of alien creepiness, it had green blood and could regenerate itself with surprising ease.

At one point in the story The Thing loses an arm. It quickly grows another, while the arm grows

left: One of the Fantastic Four, The Thing in action against Dakroth, the death demon, from Marvel comics. below: The dinosaur Triceratops.

a whole new body. Just to show that the old gothic stories had not been entirely forgotten, though, The Thing, in common with so many of its monstrous predecessors, liked nothing so much as a good drink of human blood. To everybody's relief, The Thing was eventually destroyed by electricity.

The Thing, of course, is also the name of one member of the Fantastic Four. He alone prefers to keep his real identity a secret. This is because gamma rays have changed him into a phenomenally ugly creature of immense strength. He is extremely sensitive about his orange, monster-like appearance, which is concealed from his blind girl-friend, Alicia. His real name is Ben Grimm.

Triceratops

A good description of a *TRICERATOPS* would be a cross between an elephant and a rhinoceros. Like the latter animal, it possessed a horn on the tip of its nose, but it also had two large horns or tusks which projected horizontally from its temples. This formidable armoury made it a terrible creature in battle and it is thought to be one of the few creatures who could take on

below: The Triffids on the move in 'The Day of the Triffids' originally a novel by John Wyndham.

Tyrannosaurus Rex. It was a plant eating animal and could move rather more quickly than many other dinosaurs.

Triffids

Vegetable monsters are a comparatively recent phenomenon. The most scaring and convincing were invented by the science-fiction writer John Wyndham in his novel *The Day of the Triffids*. Almost the whole population turn out to watch the passage across the sky of a large comet, the light from which is so bright that it blinds them. It is then that the *TRIFFIDS* begin to move in. They are giant, ugly plants which can uproot themselves and shuffle along the ground. They also make a sort of clattering, chattering noise with little stick-like protruberances on their bodies. Worst of all they have a single tentacle emerging from the top of their bodies. They can use this like a whip. They lash out at the blind humans and kill them, leaving a weal or burn mark on their flesh. The Triffids, it seems, can be most effectively destroyed by a flame-thrower.

Apart from the spine-chilling menace of the Triffids, the book also presents a disturbing picture of what happens to organized society when it is subjected to extraordinary circumstances. The story has been adapted for radio and was filmed in 1962.

Trog

A variation of the re-awakened monster theme was featured in the film *TROG*. A group of young potholers come across an ape-like being in an underground cave. Further investigations by a famous lady anthropologist, reveal a terrifying hairy creature partially covered in animal skins and with red-rimmed eyes. The anthropologist, played by Joan Crawford, believes the creature is a Troglodyte, or prehistoric cave dweller who has been accidentally frozen for centuries only to emerge in the twentieth century. Despite panic stricken opposition she manages to capture Trog and to cage him. She tries to humanize him but he continues to display fits of unpredictable and violent temper such as tearing an offending dog apart with his bare hands.

He is released by a man who opposes the experiments being conducted on the creature, and

above: Trog retreats to his cave carrying a small girl as captive. She is later returned unharmed.

is slaughtered for his pains. Free again, Trog runs amok and eventually retreats to his cave carrying a small girl as captive. Fortunately, the anthropologist has established enough rapport with the fiendish monster to persuade him to hand back the little girl unharmed. However, her passionate pleas cannot save him from man's wrath and his cave is sealed off forever, with Trog inside.

Tyrannosaurus Rex

TYRANNOSAURUS REX was the king of the dinosaurs. In appearance he resembled the Allosaurus but was considerably larger. He grew to some forty-five feet in length and, when balanced upright on his powerful hindlegs and tail, he was over nineteen feet tall. The head was very large and his mouth was full of razor-sharp teeth, some of which grew to the amazing length of six inches. The front legs, however, had dwindled to token arms which could not even reach the monster's own head. Tyrannosaurus Rex was extremely fierce and preyed on other dinosaurs for food. His powerful clawed feet and gigantic mouth were his best weapons and he probably used them successfully against most of his contemporaries.

overleaf: Tyrannosaurus Rex, the carnivore.

below: The fabulous Unicorn, a gentle creature.

Unicorn

Of all the magical, marvellous and monstrous beasts imagined by man, none is more alluring and attractive than the *UNICORN*. It is generally represented as a small white horse, with flowing mane and tail and, of course, with the single whorled horn which gives it its name. For centuries the Unicorn has been universally regarded as a pure and gentle creature, famed for its courage and shyness. Once however, it was thought to be extremely malevolent, and to possess a blood-chilling roar. Its beauty and the magical properties of its horn, which was an antidote to poison, probably caused people to change their mind about the Unicorn. Certainly its terrible roar was soon replaced, in legends at least, by a beautiful song which it sings when it is dying.

The lion is the traditional enemy of the Unicorn and is said to trick it into charging at a tree so that its horn becomes embedded in the trunk, thus making it an easy prey. The only human being who can exercise any power over the Unicorn is an innocent virgin. If a pure young girl is tied to a tree, the Unicorn will come and gently lay his head in her lap.

The Unicorn is an entirely mythical beast, but the tales about it are so charming and persuasive that many people wish that it actually existed. In one sense, it does because it continues to fascinate writers and artists of all kinds. Alan Garner's novel *Elidor* is one of the most recent to touch on the Unicorn legends, particularly its sad and mysterious song. All the surviving popular stories about Unicorns stress its beauty, self-sacrifice and gentleness – qualities which surely make it the most appealing monster ever.

Urisk

A shaggy-pelted, mischievous Scottish sprite is called *URISK* and is said to live in waterfalls.

Vampires

Belief in the healing or rejuvenating properties of human blood is as old as recorded history. Egyptian pharaohs who suffered from leprosy bathed in blood and this treatment was believed to cure them. The Romans maintained that blood alone could cure epilepsy. If this idea seems brutal and far-fetched to us, we should remember that the belief lingers today in symbolic form in the Christian religion. According to Christianity, the wine which is sipped during Holy Communion is a representation of Christ's blood, which cleanses and purifies.

All this may seem a long way from the legends of blood-sucking *VAMPIRES* but their history, and certainly the history of peoples' belief in them, is very closely associated with religion, particularly in Europe which is universally regarded now as the home of the vampire. Long before this, however, the Greeks believed in the *Lamiae* as blood sucking creatures and they were adopted, under the name *Stiges* by the Romans. Both the Greeks and the Romans believed in the curative properties of human blood, and both counter-balanced this 'good' belief with its opposite: the creature who thrived on human blood at the cost of human life.

Belief in vampires as members of the un-dead – creatures who rose from their graves at night to suck the blood of the living in order to sustain their ghostly life – spread throughout Central Europe during the Dark Ages and continued well into the eighteenth century. Very probably, the idea of such creatures was encouraged by the break between the Orthodox Church and that of Rome. A major point of difference between these two institutions concerned the effects of excommunication. One of the fears of excommunication was that the body

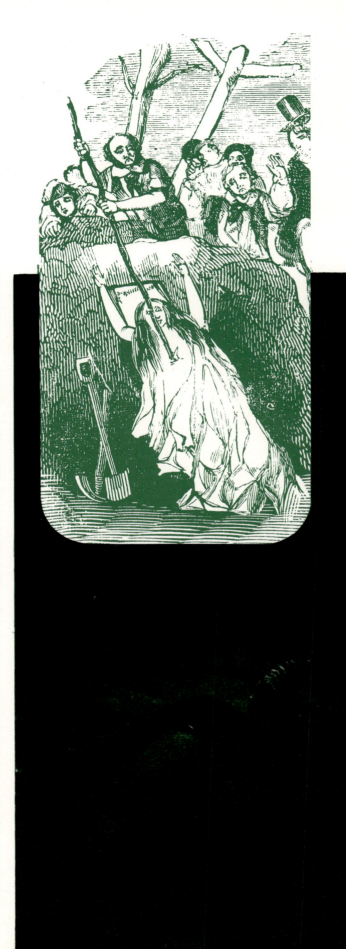

right: A stake through the heart, in a detail from 'Varney the Vampire or the Feast of Blood'.
opposite: Darkness falls and the Vampire awakes.

would not rest until the offender was received back into the Church and his soul accepted into heaven. It is probably significant that the majority of vampire stories come from countries where members of both churches lived side-by-side and where religious conflicts were commonplace.

It was believed that the bodies of excommunicated people, and those who died without receiving absolution, did not decompose in their graves. Many incidences have been recorded of graves being opened weeks, months and even years after burial only to reveal fresh corpses which, when beheaded, let out a stream of fresh blood. These graves were opened, of course, because their inhabitants had been accused of vampirism. Often the corpses of the un-dead were found to have blood on their faces and hands. This was taken as proof of vampirism but another explanation is that it was the result of premature burial. Burial of the living could easily occur when so little was known about life and death and medical science was, at best, a haphazard affair.

Whatever the explanation of the legends of fresh corpses, at the time people believed implicitly in vampires. These restless creatures rose from their graves at night and bit the necks of the living in order to drink their blood. Once bitten by a vampire, the victim automatically became infected,

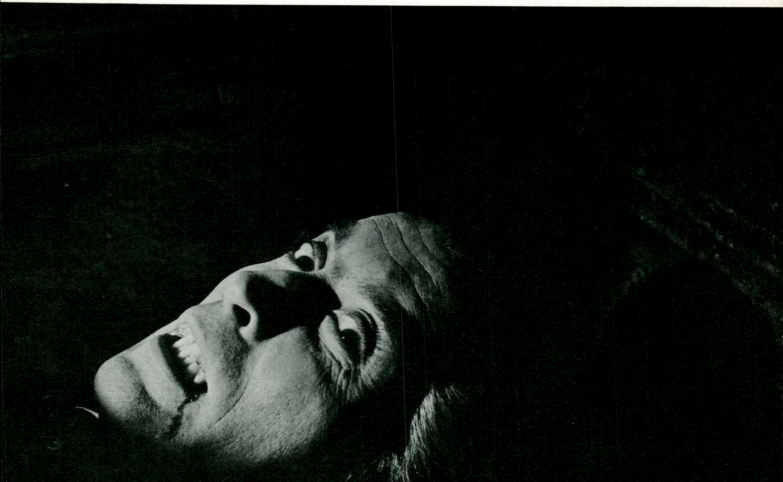

as it were, and became a vampire himself. The victims invariably felt that they were suffocating and soon fell into a trance-like state from which they never recovered.

The most completely documented and most often quoted vampire story occurred in a small village on the borders of Austria and Hungary in about 1720. Late one night, a young soldier was sitting with the landlord and his son. An old man entered the house and sat down at the table. The father and his son appeared to be frightened out of their wits by the old man who, after a while, put his face to the neck of the man and then left. The next day the landlord was found dead in bed and the boy told the soldier that the visitor was his grandfather who had been dead for ten years! The young soldier reported this story to his commanding officer who ordered an official investigation. They found much verbal evidence of vampirism in the village and, on opening the graves of the long-dead grandfather and others accused of vampirism, they found the bodies undecayed. Indeed, according to reports they looked as though they had only just been buried.

In some places during the eighteenth century a sort of vampire witch-hunt began. Not content with accusations from victims, graveyards were searched for likely culprits. The search was made by an innocent young boy mounted on a jet black horse which he rode through the graveyard. Any grave over which the horse refused to jump was said to contain a vampire. Of course, all reports of this practice claim that when the offending graves were opened, they were always found to contain fresh and bloody corpses.

It is generally believed that vampires can only be vanquished by having wooden stakes driven through their hearts, but other means of dealing with these creatures are reported. In Bavaria the body was decapitated. In Crete the head of the un-dead corpse was boiled in vinegar, and in many countries it was usual to drive nails through the head in addition to the stake through the heart. Garlic was an almost universal protection against vampiric onslaughts, except in Spain where there was said to be no known remedy!

The vampire is now almost completely associated with Count *Dracula* who has been eternally popularized by Bram Stoker and many films. It is

above: An illustration from "Varny the Vampire".

interesting, not to say uncanny, to note that the first major literary version of the Central European vampire legend was written as a contribution to the same ghost story competition which produced Mary Shelley's immortal *Frankenstein*. Dr John William Polidori was a friend of Lord Byron and of the Shelleys and that fateful summer in Switzerland he wrote a story called *The Vampire* which appeared in 1819 under Lord Byron's name. Since the inspiration of these stories was a collection of German ghost stories, it is perhaps not surprising that Polidori should have chosen vampirism as his subject. What is remarkable is that two of the most durable monster creations should have emerged in book form at the same time.

Fact and fiction concerning Dracula and vampires are now so closely intermingled that it is very difficult to separate one from the other. We can point with some certainty, however, to the existence of a real life vampire. Known as the

left: More evil than Dracula is Warner Bros 'Blacula', a vampire from 1972, about to bite.

'Bloody Countess' and as the 'Tigress of Csejthe' – the name of her castle in Hungary – Elisabeth Bathory lived at the end of the sixteenth and in the early part of the seventeenth centuries. She was a very beautiful and very cruel woman. More than anything she feared growing old and losing her beauty. She was also very superstitious and was greatly influenced by the advice and predictions of the sorceresses she kept in her employment. During her childhood Elisabeth Bathory was a victim of epilepsy and it is interesting to speculate whether the ancient Roman 'cure' was administered to her. Whatever the initial cause, Elisabeth Bathory believed that the blood of young virgins alone would keep her young and beautiful. And a terrible story told of how she came to believe this.

Always a woman of violent temper, she one day hit her maid so hard that the girl's nose bled and spattered the Countess' face with blood. When she wiped these spots away, Elisabeth thought that they had improved her complexion, and so her reign of terror began. Eventually she was believed to have tortured and killed six hundred and fifty young women in order to take her grisly blood baths at four o'clock each morning. She was aided and abetted by equally cruel and unscrupulous servants, one of whom was indirectly her undoing in the end.

When, in spite of her superstitious beliefs, the Countess continued to age, one of her advisers said that she must bathe in the blue blood of young aristocratic girls. At that time in Hungary, the authorities took no notice of stories about the mutilated bodies of peasant girls and certainly would not believe these rumours against the word of a noble Countess. But when well-born young women began to disappear, they decided to investigate. In 1611, Elisabeth Bathory's servants and helpers were charged with the torture and slaughter of six hundred and fifty girls over a period of many years. The Countess herself was never formally charged nor did she appear in court. Her high birth and important political connections protected her. Instead she was imprisoned in her own castle and forbidden any contact with the outside world. She died there, old, alone and ugly, three years after the discovery of her mass murders.

Elisabeth Bathory was certainly a vampire in the sense that she believed that she needed the pure blood of young women to keep her alive and beautiful. Her story has greatly influenced vampire legend and will continue to do so. For most people, however, the word 'vampire' conjures up a picture of Dracula or of a bat. The association of bats with hell and all things evil is very old indeed, and bats are certainly exploited by Bram Stoker in his novel. The earliest vampire film portrayed the Devil transformed into a black, blood-sucking bat. Several species of bats, mostly resident in South America, are believed to be blood drinking. They do not suck the blood, however, but are said to lap it from a superficial wound. It is more probable that the so-called vampire bats have had these habits wished upon them from the legends – but in the absence of any real proof it is obviously wise to keep out of their way!

left: The Vampire carries off his swooning victim in The Vampire (United Artists 1957) right: The age old remedy of the brandished Crucifix shrivels Christopher Lee as Count Dracula.

Vodyany

The Slav people had their own water spirits who lived in crystal palaces at the bottom of lakes, rivers and especially mill ponds. These palaces were ornamented with treasure taken from sunken boats and were lit by a magic stone, which it is said, shone more brightly than the sun itself. The inhabitants of these fabulous underwater palaces were called *VODYANY* and they kept human beings as slaves. Since they loved rushing water, they were always destroying dams and interfering with mill-wheels. They also hated people and would snatch bathers down to their crystal lairs, and even pull people from the land to drown in their watery homes. Vodyany were semi-human in appearance, but very ugly. Their bodies were often covered with moss and weed and their eyes were red. Some had long green hair, and others beards which changed colour when the moon waned. Many had long horns, tails and very large paws. Vodyany slept during the day but loved to splash about on the surface of the water at night. They made a great deal of noise and anyone who was foolish enough to go and investigate invariably met a watery death and an after-life of slavery.

Vritra

The exceptionally rich mythology of India includes the tale of a monster named *VRITRA*. Vritra was especially created to challenge Indra, the king of the gods, who had destroyed the son of a powerful Brahman. Vritra was a demon so large that his head touched the sky. He challenged Indra to a long and bloody battle. At last, he seized Indra, pushed him into his enormous mouth and swallowed him. The other gods decided to gag the monster, who opened his mouth to terrify them. Indra, seizing his opportunity, leapt free of the monster's mouth and the battle began again. Indra, however, was eventually forced to retreat and he then made a pact with Vritra. The monster promised to leave him alone as long as Indra promised not to kill him. To make doubly sure, Vritra said he must promise never to kill him with any of the known substances from which weapons were made. In fact, Indra broke his promise. The god Vishnu turned himself into a magic foam column and Indra killed Vritra.

Vulture

A film which cleverly combines ancient legends of supernatural revenge with the manufacturing of modern science fiction monsters begins with a young woman seeing a vast bird of prey with a human head apparently rising from the grave of a man who is said to have been buried alive some two hundred years before. This is the *VULTURE*. Despite the evidence of an empty grave with a large black feather beside it, the girl's evident shock, and a parchment in the hand of the dead man vowing to return from the grave to wreak his vengeance, no one believes the girl's story. Soon a hacked and mutilated sheep is found – obviously the prey of some monstrous creature. Eventually we learn that a mad professor has transformed himself into a man-sized Vulture with the aid of nuclear energy. He is using the legend as a cover-up for his own nefarious schemes. He seizes the unfortunate heroine in his man-sized talons and carries her off to his mountain eyrie. She manages to seize a revolver, however, and shoots the horrible man-bird.

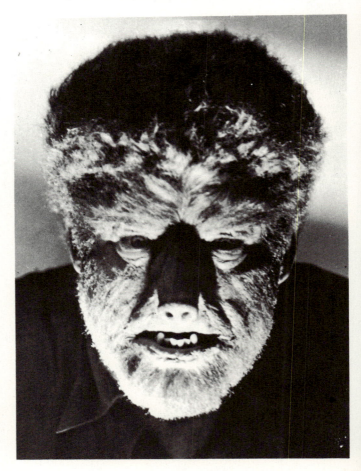

Werewolf

What makes the *WEREWOLF* so terrifying is that it is a man who not only changes himself into the shape of a wolf but also takes on the savage nature of the animal. Werewolves roam the countryside in search of human victims whom they kill and partially devour. The werewolf (literally man-wolf) is particularly fond of human blood.

Legends of werewolves have been taken very seriously. So seriously, in fact, that a special scientific term – *lycanthropy* – is used to describe the condition. Not surprisingly, legends about werewolves, or *lycanthropes* flourished at a time and in countries where wolves were found in abundance. During the harsh winters of Medieval Europe, these savage beasts would prey on human beings and the natural fear of them, together with observation of their habits reinforced the belief in men and even women who could transform themselves into stalking werewolves.

In France in 1547 a man named Gilles Garnier was executed for being a werewolf. Garnier

left: The spine-chilling stare of the Wolf Man.
below: Oliver Reed has a change of character and of role in 'The Curse of the Werewolf', Hammer.

certainly murdered several children and in most peculiar circumstances. He is said to have dragged a girl into the woods by his teeth and to have eaten a large part of her. At his trial Garnier agreed with witnesses who had seen him commit another murder that he had then been in human form, but he always maintained that he was a wolf when perpetuating his other crimes.

The trial and execution of Gilles Garnier show how seriously the werewolf was taken. Since then a number of learned doctors and psychologists have seriously investigated the idea that a man might be so convinced that he is a wolf that he can come to behave like one. This might explain certain bestial murders, although there is still no evidence of a real bodily change.

As usual with legends, there are varying descriptions of the habits and appearance of werewolves. Many claim that the man is literally transformed into a wolf and that he will then dig up newly buried corpses in order to satisfy his blood-lust. This, of course, may be based on actual occurences – for real wolves, if sufficiently hungry,

will 'open' recent graves in order to feed. The superstitious mind could easily believe that this was the work of a werewolf.

The most popular werewolf stories, however, explain the transformation as a curse or spell. Unlike *vampires* werewolves are reluctant victims of some evil enchantment. At full moon, and quite involuntarily, their hands become hairy, their nails turn into strong claws and they grow wolf-like fangs. The werewolf can only be killed by pure silver, usually in the form of a special silver bullet, or the silver head of a cane.

It is this rather reluctant half-man/half-wolf that has regularly been featured in films. The earliest cinematic werewolves were based on American legends and used real wolves to 'play' the transformed human being. It was soon discovered, though, that a well made-up actor, part man and part slavering wolf, made a more effective movie monster. Lon Chaney was probably the most famous of the cinema's blood-thirsty and blood-curdling werewolves, although many people argue that Oliver Reed was the most frightening of them all.

The werewolf is certainly a spectacular and sinister monster, but it is also important because it shows how the strangest stories can have a basis in psychological if not physical reality.

left: The lady screams in horror when faced with the Teenage Werewolf. below: The Werewolf stalks abroad at night, searching for his prey.

Worm of Lambton

Like many ancient folk stories, that concerning the horrible *WORM OF LAMBTON* has an obvious moral. Centuries ago the young heir of Lambton was a pleasure loving man who preferred to go fishing on Sunday rather than to church. On one of these Sunday fishing trips he hooked a large ugly lizard-like creature, with nine holes around its mouth. The young man dropped the creature down a deep well. Shortly afterwards he left England to fight in a Crusade. The Worm grew and grew into a vast serpentine creature which left the well and took up residence on a nearby hill. It would wrap its scaley coils around this hill and prey upon sheep and cattle. When it had devoured all the livestock in the immediate area, it went to attack Lambton Hall. The residents of that place kept it at bay by feeding it the milk of nine cows in a great trough each day. Several knights tried to kill the Worm, during this time but they all failed, largely because the Worm could join itself magically together again when cut in two, or when any part of it was lopped off.

At last the young heir who had brought this misfortune on his home returned, a reformed character, and determined to kill the greedy Worm. He sought the advice of a 'wise woman' who said that he must have metal spikes fixed all over his armour and that he must fight the monster in the middle of the river. In addition, he had to vow to kill the first living creature he saw after slaying the Worm. If he failed in this, his family would be cursed for nine generations.

The heir did exactly as the wise woman said. The Worm immediately attacked him, twining its sinuous body about his armour. The spikes thus drove into the monster's body, wounding it deeply. Meanwhile, the heir hacked away at it with his sword. The fast flowing river carried each hacked off piece of the creature away before it had time to join itself together again. After a long and bloody struggle, the heir overcame the Worm.

He had decided to fulfill his promise by slaughtering his favourite dog. Accordingly, he had arranged for the dog to be let loose when he blew his horn to announce his triumph over the Worm. However, his father, anxious at the long absence of his son, had set off for the river and was the first living creature he saw. The heir blew his horn again for the dog which came rushing towards him. He killed it but he had not obeyed the wise woman to the letter and his family was cursed for nine generations.

below: The Abominable Snowman's footprint?

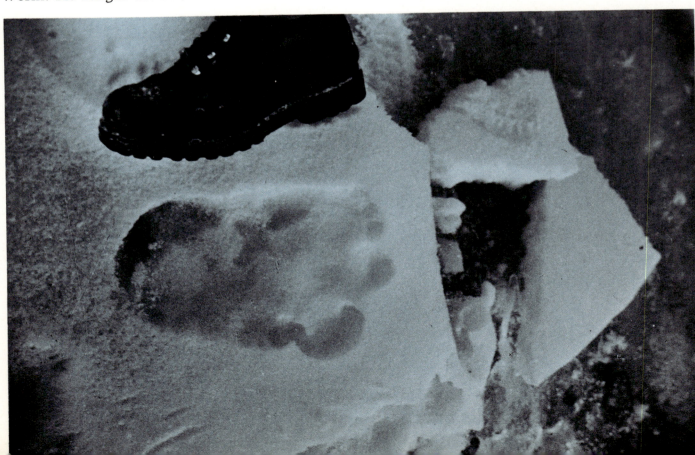

Yena

The scavenging hyena was undoubtedly once mistaken for a monstrous beast called the *YENA*, around which many legends grew. In the twelfth century it was described in a book of animals or bestiary as having a completely rigid backbone so that it was unable to turn around quickly. Even

to have the trick of imitating human speech exactly, which it did to lure human prey. Perhaps in connection with this strange ability it could deprive hunting dogs of their voices and even paralyse them by running round them three times. It was also believed that the Yena carried a stone in its eye which, if removed and placed in the man's mouth, enabled him to see the future.

Yeti

It was in 1951, as a direct result of the extraordinary discoveries of the pathfinding or reconnaisance party for the British Everest expedition of 1953, that the *YETI* or Abominable Snowman hit the headlines and secured a place for itself in both the public and the scientific

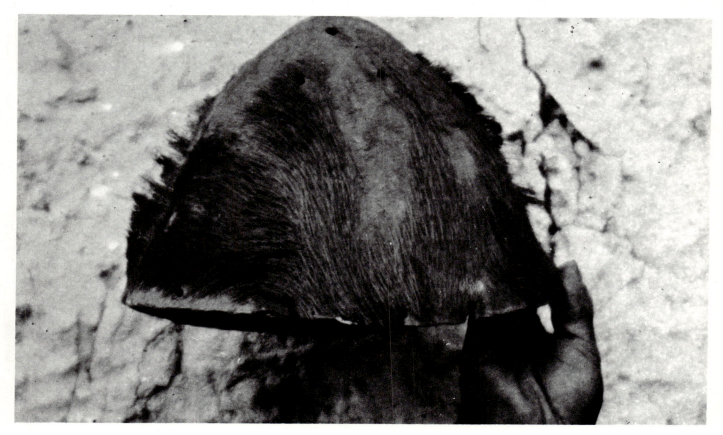

more surprisingly, it could change its sex at will and so came to be regarded as a symbol of inconstancy. The Yena liked to live in the tombs of the dead and to feed on corpses. When it was unable to do this it would dig up graves and devour their contents.

Like its actual prototype, the Yena's voice resembled that of a human being, but it was said

above: The so-called Pangboche scalp, discovered in the Himalayas. Is this evidence of a Yeti?

imagination. A member of that reconnaisance party, Eric Shipton, photographed a footprint in the snow at 18,000 feet. The print was large and clearly showed the impress of five toes. It was, if not human, then certainly humanoid. It indicated the presence in the upper reaches of the Himalayas of a large, heavy creature that walked on two feet.

Because of the publicity received by this discovery, and the emergence of the popular name Abominable Snowman, the fact that the photograph only seemed to confirm stories that had been circulating for years has been forgotten. As long ago as 1887, footprints of a similar kind were observed and described by a European. The Everest expedition of 1921 recorded mysterious tracks in the snow and Sir John Hunt himself noted similar tracks in 1937. Indeed it would take a book to list all the sightings, both European and native, the majority of which tally to a remarkable degree.

One particularly unusual occurrence is worth recording. In 1942, a Polish refugee, escaping with a group of fellow prisoners of mixed nationality from a Siberian labour camp, crossed part of the Himalayas and saw two Yetis on a high ledge. These creatures were described as being eight feet tall and resembled a cross between a bear and an orang-outang. They were covered in long hair, except for their faces, and moved habitually on two legs.

As a result of the publicity given to the Everest expedition of 1953, the 'Daily Mail', London, sponsored a special Yeti expedition in 1954. This was made up of scientists, film-makers and climbers and was solely concerned to discover as much as possible about the Yeti.

The name 'Yeti' is a corruption of the Sherpa name, 'Yeh-Teh'. 'Yeh' means 'rocky place' and 'Teh' is simply the Sherpa word for this particular animal. There are, however, two notably different sorts of 'Teh'. The 'Dzu-Teh' is the larger kind and is believed to prey on cattle. The Sherpas themselves accept that this is a local name for the Himalayan bear, common in Tibet, but occasionally encountered in Nepal. The other type of 'Yeh-Teh' is the smaller 'Mih-Teh', meaning man-Teh. It does not prey on cattle and is associated with man. Nobody is quite sure whether this association refers to the creature's man-like appearance, or means that it is dangerous to man. Probably the name 'Mih-Teh' encompasses both ideas. The reliable sightings recorded, all stress the Yeti's man-like appearance and most Sherpas are afraid of the creature, although it does not appear to attack them.

The 'Mih-Teh' then, is the creature we know as the Yeti. Before the 1954 Yeti hunt, many people said that the creature was either the Himalayan bear or the langur monkey. Examination of the local language shows that the Sherpas are well aware of the existence of the bear, the 'Dzu-Teh' and of the langur monkey which they never confuse with the Yeti proper. The langur monkey is tree-dwelling, quite distinctly marked and has a long tail. It in no way resembles descriptions of the Yeti which is, in any case, always sighted above the tree-line.

As with the Loch Ness Monster it is possible, by piecing together the various sightings, to arrive at a general description of the Yeti. It seems to average about five feet six inches in height – about the size of a small man. It is covered all over in reddish brown hair, which is usually said to grow in profusion on its head, although the face is hairless. The head is noticeably pointed in shape. It has no tail and, as we know from the famous footprint, it has a distinctly humanoid, five-toed foot. The Yeti usually walks upright, but eye-witnesses maintain that it will drop on to all fours when it is in a hurry. Tracks have confirmed this alternative mode of walking. The Yeti has a high-pitched, mewling cry. It appears to be harmless to man, although evidence on this point is confused. Its very sudden and unexpected appearance has often frightened Sherpa observers who may, therefore, attribute aggressive instincts to it. Others, particularly monks and priests from the many monasteries in the Himalayas, attribute considerable intelligence to the creature which, they say, is curious about man but rather timid of him. The evidence suggests that the Yeti will leave man alone as long as he returns the compliment. This is certainly the attitude adopted by most Sherpas.

There is other physical evidence pointing to the Yeti's existence, if not now, at some time in the past. In 1954 a group of Indian climbers were shown a Yeti scalp at the Buddhist monastery of Pangboche. It was large and conical in shape. Quite a lot of hair was present despite the extreme age of the scalp – an estimated three hundred years. The hair grows in a similar way to that of man. The skin of this scalp is extremely thick. The Pangboche scalp was later seen by members of the Yeti expedition from England. They discovered that although it is not a sacred relic, it does play a part in local religious ritual and the monks refused to loan it for scientific examination. Hairs were obtained from the scalp and these, after scientific analysis, were found at the time to correspond to those of no known animal.

A second scalp was discovered by the Yeti hunters at Khumjung monastery. This was similar in every way and again the expedition failed to borrow it. In compensation however, they were given a small fragment of Yeti skin which corresponds in colour and appearance to the descriptions we have of the creature. Later however, it was proved that both scalps were in fact made from the hide of the 'serow', a Himalayan goat-antelope. The monasteries were unable to shed any light on the matter.

Perhaps the most convincing evidence concerning the Yeti is the unquestioned belief in its existence held by the Sherpas. The Sherpas are not a primitive race, although they have been isolated from the rest of the world for many years. Most important of all is the fact that they do not regard the Yeti as a special or fantastic animal in any way. They were, it is reported, surprised to learn that there were no Yetis in other parts of the world. They accept that it is seldom seen because it is a nomadic animal and lives in a remote and difficult terrain. In other words the Yeti, to the native Sherpas, is a rare, but in no way extraordinary animal.

At approximately 17,000 feet the snowline of the Himalayas begins. Above that line the mountains are perpetually snow-covered. Between the edge of the snow and the beginning of the treeline, the forested area, at about 13,000 feet, is a vast region of rocky country, pitted with gorges and valleys. It is here that the Yeti is believed to live, here that its tracks and occasional droppings have been found. Since we may assume that a 'forgotten' animal will only exist in small numbers, it would be very easy for creatures to live there without being sighted. Not only are there thousands of miles in which to hide, but the terrain is largely unexplored and full of hiding places. It is, however, well populated with smaller animals, rodents etc. on which the Yeti is believed to feed.

It also seems certain that the Yeti is a nomadic or roaming creature. This is indicated by the fact that it is most commonly seen in winter when the snows drive it lower down the mountains in search of food. It would also explain the infrequency of sightings, would suggest that they are few in number and is reinforced by the fact that, as hunters of smaller animals, they would need to keep on the move.

below: The tracks of the Yeti in the snow?

Z

Zombies

According to Caribbean Voodoo superstition newly-dead corpses can be reanimated and made to serve the will of a powerful mind. These creatures which lack souls or wills of their own are called *ZOMBIES*, the walking dead. As monsters, zombies have been very popular in films where they usually behave like sleep-walking automatons forced to do the dirty work of some evil master.

Early films such as *White Zombie* generally stuck to the West Indian origins of the zombie, having the creature revived by elaborate voodoo ceremonies. With the growing popularity of science-fiction, however, many zombies were revived by quasi-scientific means, including the use of super-powers from outer space. In horror movies, the un-dead qualities of zombies are obviously borrowed from vampire legends, while their re-animation invariably recalls Frankenstein's story. Lacking souls, they are thought to be capable of great evil, and their short stay in their graves provides marvellous opportunities for make-up artists to let their imaginations run riot through the various stages of ugly decomposition.

below: The White Zombie was revived by Voodoo.

Index